JUN 27 1995

J
793.8
BLA

Blackstone, Harry.
200 magic tricks
anyone can do

WITHDRAWN

WARRENVILLE PUBLIC LIBRARY DISTRICT
28W751 Stafford Place
Warrenville, IL 60555

200 MagicTricks
Anyone Can Do

HARRY BLACKSTONE

200 MAGIC TRICKS
ANYONE CAN DO

Introduction by Walter Gibson

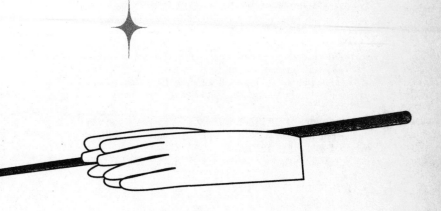

WINGS BOOKS
New York • Avenel, New Jersey

WARRENVILLE PUBLIC LIBRARY

Copyright © 1983 by Walter Gibson

All rights reserved. No part of this book may be reproduced in any form, except by a newspaper or magazine reviewer who wishes to quote brief passages in connection with a review.

This 1995 edition is published by Wings Books, distributed by Random House Value Publishing, Inc., 40 Engelhard Avenue, Avenel, New Jersey 07001, by arrangement with Carol Publishing Group.

Random House
New York • Toronto • London • Sydney • Auckland

Printed and bound in the United States of America

Library of Congress Cataloging-in-Publication Data

Blackstone, Harry.
    [Tricks anyone can do]
    200 magic tricks anyone can do / Harry Blackstone; introduction by Walter Gibson.
            p.   cm.
    Originally published: Blackstone's tricks anyone can do / Harry Blackstone. New York, NY : Carol Pub. Group, 1983.
    ISBN 0-517-12359-2
    1. Conjuring.   2. Tricks.   I. Title.   II. Title: Two hundred magic tricks anyone can do.
GV1547.B644   1995
793.8—dc20   94-41614
                                                                    CIP

8 7 6 5 4 3 2 1

BLACKSTONE, MASTER OF MAGIC

Today, the name of Blackstone is so symbolic of Magic that to most people, as far back as they can remember, the two were one and the same. Naturally, like all great results, this had a small beginning, but it's growth was so steady and so impressive that within the next decade it will pass the century mark. That alone is magical – to think that the wonderment of the Gaslight Era could be carried into the Space Age – but when you consider the skill and inventive genius that bearers of the name Blackstone have applied to the field of mystery, the answer becomes self-evident.

The "small beginning" was represented by a twelve-year-old

boy who had saved his small change to buy a gallery seat at the McVickers Theatre in Chicago to witness a magical performance by Harry Kellar, who had become America's leading magician. This was in 1897 and the boy, like very many others, left the theatre, vowing that he, too, would some day become a master of magic. With most, for a variety of reasons, that turned out to be an idle wish, but this boy, whose name was Harry Bouton, made it a constant dream. He learned all he could from library books on magic, practicing tricks with cards, coins and other objects that required various degrees of skill, until he became quite adept at sleight-of-hand.

Meanwhile, he worked at jobs that proved equally helpful toward a magical career. From cabinet makers and other craftsmen, he learned skills that enabled him to construct his own magical apparatus along the lines explained in books. In this, he was aided by his brother Pete, who was a mechanical genius in his own right and solved many technical details while Harry was watching magical acts to learn the types and trends that the audiences liked most. He found that some preferred to watch skilled specialists perform deft sleights and others were impressed by large stage illusions, presented on a lavish scale.

So Harry Bouton decided to go for both and at the same time inject surprise features that fitted in between. In this, he was guided to a marked degree by his famous namesake, Harry Kellar, as future events were to prove. For all during the years that marked the shaping of his own magical career, Harry Bouton never lost sight of the goal that gripped him when he viewed the Great Kellar show from the gallery of the McVickers Theatre. He knew that Kellar had reached the top step by step, so he proceeded to do the same.

The first step was to produce a vaudeville act that would

meet the growing demand for novelty, so by 1904 the Bouton Brothers appeared under the billing of "Straight and Crooked Magic," in which Harry performed new and effective tricks in true magical style, while Pete, as his comedy assistant, tried to copy them, only to have them fail and leave him totally frustrated and nonplussed. This act scored a real hit over the growing vaudeville circuits during the next few years, until several assistants and large illusions were added to form a head-line attraction under the name of Harry Bouton and Company.

Continuing success in vaudeville led to further expansion, until the time was ripe to embark upon a full evening road-show with a much larger company and still more equipment. In planning this venture, Harry decided to adopt a name that would be remembered more easily than his own. The name he chose was Blackstone, and it captured the public from the start. It also marked the attainment of an ambition, for this was the type of show that the Great Kellar had headed; and as the Great Blackstone, Harry felt worthy of their mutual name.

That ambition was doubly realized when the Blackstone show made its first tour to the West Coast and appeared in Los Angeles. Among the audience which came to see the brilliant young magician was an elderly gentleman long retired from the stage, who was so intrigued by Blackstone's performance that he wanted to meet him and extend his congratulations. The enthusiastic gentleman was none other than the Great Kellar himself.

To Blackstone, that visit was the greatest thrill in his life, approached only by the occasion when as a boy, he had seen Kellar for the first time. Yet Kellar was even happier. He, the Great Wizard of the Past, had found the man he was confident would become the Master Magician of the Future. During the few remaining years of Kellar's life, he and Blackstone were inseparable whenever they could find occasion to be together. Kellar delved deeply into the choicest secrets of his art so that Blackstone might carry on the traditions which he, Kellar, had earlier established.

At that time, Kellar was working to perfect his greatest illusion, the "Levitation of Princess Karnac," which he had performed on the stage, but had improved after his retirement. Before he died, Kellar left instructions that the Levitation should be given to Blackstone. That order was fulfilled and the modern miracle of the Floating Princess became an outstanding feature of the Great Blackstone show.

During the years that followed World War I, the show itself grew larger and became so famous that with the outbreak of World War II, the United Service Organization called upon Blackstone to present his full show at Army camps and Navy bases throughout the United States. The U.S.O. was such a success, that after the War, Blackstone, with his brother Pete Bouton and a company of thirty, resumed his tours of the larger cities in the United States and Canada, until, after a professional career of well over fifty years, he retired to California in 1960 and died there, five years later.

All the while, the Great Blackstone had remembered those meetings with Kellar and how ardently he had worked to learn magic in his boyhood. By the year 1929, as a help to others who sought the same path, he produced a popular book entitled *Blackstone's Secrets of Magic,* which promptly became a classic in its field and was followed a few years later by *Blackstone's Modern Card Tricks,* which also became so popular that the two were later combined in a single volume.

During the twenty years that followed, Blackstone contributed more tricks to magical magazines, his own show books, comic books and similar publications, as well as his own radio show; and in 1949, to mark his twentieth year of authorship, he chose special items from those books and other sources to compose the very volume that he would have welcomed instantly back in those early days. Its title, *Blackstone's Tricks Anyone Can Do*, should sound familiar, because it is the very book that you will be reading as you turn the pages that follow. Back in print, after another forty years, it will acquaint you with the methods of time-tested magic that only the Great Blackstone could provide.

WALTER GIBSON

HARRY BLACKSTONE, AMERICA'S PREMIER PRESTIDIGITATOR

Every time that Harry Blackstone steps on stage for a performance of a grand and glorious edition of The Blackstone Magic Show, he brings with him the precious legacy of an American theatrical tradition that dates back nearly eighty years.

Named "Magician of the Year, 1979" by The Academy of Magical Arts, the gifted son and professional heir of The Great Blackstone, America's legendary creative magical genius, is currently involved in a far more ambitious undertaking than merely following in his father's giant footsteps.

"The Great Blackstone led the art of stage magic and illusion to heights never before reached," Harry believes.

Looking closely at the background and experience of Blackstone, in the years prior to the dramatic debut of what *Newsweek* termed "the largest and most spectacular traveling magic show ever," you get the distinct impression that each and every professional involvement in his career provided pertinent "basic training" in the complex skills necessary to the creation, staging and cross-continental touring of an elaborate stage spectacular.

Harry Blackstone, Jr., began his magical career at the age of six months — appearing and disappearing from his famous father's illusions. By age four, he was performing feats of "mental telepathy" for visitors to the Blackstones' Michigan home. When he first performed it, he even astonished his mother and father: he'd learned their complicated code while eavesdropping on rehearsals!

When he was seven, Harry, Jr. was on the road with his father's celebrated illusion show. His mother, Billie, was her husband's number one assistant, and Pete Bouton, Harry, Jr.'s uncle, was technical director of the large touring show.

Under the watchful eye of his father and uncle, Harry learned, by trial and error, the elements of his craft. All the world-famous Blackstone illusions — the Floating Light Bulb, Dancing Handkerchief, Vanishing Birdcage, even the terrifying Buzz-saw — were mastered by the young man while Harry, Sr. and Uncle Pete critiqued and encouraged him.

During his late teens, young Harry decided that, rather than carry on the family show, he would specialize in something else — perhaps acting or theatre administration.

Harry enrolled in Swarthmore College, later transferring to the University of Southern California and the University of Texas for majors in theatre arts. He joined the Army shortly after graduation and because of college training in Oriental languages, was assigned to Japan. While in the land of cherry blossoms he became the first Occidental to appear in an all-Japanese stage production, *The Teahouse of the August Moon.*

Mustered out of the Army, Harry entered graduate school at the University of Texas in Austin. He obtained a part-time job at a local TV station, owned by then-U.S. Senator Lyndon B. Johnson and his wife, Lady Bird. Needing a magician for a commercial he was producing, Harry did the job himself. The spot was quite successful and Harry was soon performing on a local children's TV show and was often asked to entertain at parties at the LBJ Ranch. At one of the gatherings, a guest sought him out after the show and encouraged him to consider re-entering, full-time, the world of magic. A well-received engagement at Las Vegas' Tropicana Hotel soon followed and offers poured in. Harry accepted as many as possible but was not yet fully convinced that his destiny was, indeed, that of a professional magician.

Pursuing his TV experience, Harry joined the Smothers Brothers in an important production post on their CBS-TV variety show. This led to the highly responsible job of managing three West Coast companies of the smash-hit Broadway musical, *Hair.* And, he produced for the Smothers Brothers an acclaimed Las Vegas act.

The Great Blackstone died in 1965. After that time, many of his father's former associates continually urged Harry to return, full time, to magic.

"I heard them and I understood what they were saying but, for many reasons, I resisted," Harry remembers. "Finally, one day, a light went on in the back of my head. It said: 'Do it!' I resolved then and there to do everything within my power to continue and enhance the name Blackstone and all that it stands for in the worlds of magic and entertainment."

When the magic fraternity heard the news that Harry had made his decision, calls began coming in from across the world. Former assistants to his father offered help; technical experts who had worked with Harry, Sr. sent plans for illusions that had been created but never constructed. It was as if the entire world of magic was cheering for the young man with the awesome task — the responsibility for re-introducing to America the name Blackstone as a synonym for all that is wondrous, exciting and magnificent in the world of illusion!

"Another wonderful thing happened to convice me that I was on the right road," Harry says. "I met a beautiful young lady named Gay Blevins and she began working as my assistant. Now she is my partner, my wife, my strongest critic and one of the constant, positive forces in my life and work."

With Gay involved every step of the way, the past few years have seen Harry Blackstone emerge as the world's most famous magician. After several years of headlining top night clubs, hotels and television shows all over the world, in 1978 his dream at last came true: Harry Blackstone, Jr., conceived and mounted the largest illusion show that the world has seen since his father's retirement.

"It is what my father always dreamed of for me", Harry says. "It took 40 years of my life and work to reach the time that was exactly right for me to attempt it."

The word was out: The Blackstone Magic Show is back again, bigger and better than ever!

"The response has been most gratifying," says Harry sincerely. "I am particularly pleased that audiences and reviewers are accepting me on my own terms. My father was The Great Blackstone and he will always be remembered and revered. Though he taught me countless things, I am my own man and this is *our,* 1980's style Blackstone Magic Show. I'm very proud of it — and think that he would be, too."

Officially named as America's Bicentennial Magician in 1976, Harry was one of two Americans invited to perform before Queen Elizabeth II at her Silver Jubilee Gala at Windsor Castle. Recently he was awarded the Star of Magic, an honor bestowed only eleven times in eighty years. The Great Blackstone also received this award over thirty years ago.

PREFACE

THIS BOOK IS INTENDED AS A HANDY AND COMPACT GUIDE to the fascinating art of magic, in which I have revelled for many years and from which I hope others will gain the same enjoyment, once they have practiced the tricks and methods explained in this volume.

Every year, magic is gaining greater popularity because it offers more reward than any other hobby. The time spent learning tricks, practicing them and working out individual notions, is a pastime in itself. Yet that is the mere preliminary to the later test of public presentation, the final goal of every magician.

The right way to learn magic is to begin by doing it, since all results depend upon the reaction of your audience. Hence the beginner can pick a few easy tricks, try them, and proceed with more difficult methods as he goes along. Yet he will find, during the process, that the simpler tricks he learned first will improve with his own study of advanced methods and the development of his own technique.

In selecting the material for this book, I have purposely chosen tested items that the reader will find sure-fire. To these I have added tricks that will provide a distinct touch of novelty. I have also taken a wide range of material so that the reader can add variety to his program as he builds it.

Card tricks constitute a considerable portion of the volume and in describing them, I have gone into the subject of preliminary sleights involving skill entirely within the ability of the average reader. Where cards are concerned, a person should first learn to handle a pack smoothly, devoting some time to ordinary shuffling and dealing, after which the acquisition of simple sleights will become a matter of course.

The same rule applies to some degree with all tricks. In handling any objects—coins, ropes, handkerchiefs or whatever else instructions call for—the reader should cultivate a deft, convincing style. To become a magician, it is necessary to act the part of a magician, and therein lies the great fun of magic.

With these notes, I am starting the reader on his way to learn by actual experience the proof of my sayings. The first chapter will introduce some novel stunts that will in turn prove steps to further trickery. From then on, you, the reader, will be the magician.

HARRY BLACKSTONE

CONTENTS

Chapter 1

BAFFLERS

As an introductory route to trickery and magic, these "Bafflers" will be found ideal. The term is applied to those perplexing problems which start out as impossibilities but wind up with a trick solution requiring a demonstration.

Admittedly, such "Bafflers" are on the borderland of puzzles, since their solution must be given in order to make them valid. But they come into the realm of tricks, since they must be performed as such. This in turn requires presentation, which is the basis of all magic.

If you can fool your friends with "Bafflers" up to the climax of each stunt, you are in a fair way toward becoming an impromptu magician. Your next step is to give them the same hocus-pocus with other simple tricks that remain unsolved when their demonstration is completed. You will find many such tricks in the later chapters.

The further you go, the more magic you will know; but even when you have long passed the beginner stage, you will find your old friends, the "Bafflers," still suitable and worthy of performance, particularly as interludes to spice more ambitious experiments in the art of friendly deception.

You will have to try out these "Bafflers" too, if only in

self-protection against the time when you are versed in magic. Nobody likes anything better than to "catch" a magician with some bit of trivial trickery, hence you will need to be fortified for the game of "Catch as Catch Can" to come right back at your rivals.

1. THE MIGHTY MATCH Invert two drinking glasses on the table and place a match horizontally between their slanted sides, so that it is held in place by the pressure of the glasses.

The problem then is to turn over one of the glasses without having the match fall from its position. Sure failure will result when anyone tries the trick—until you demonstrate the secret method.

Light another match and set it to the head of the match that is between the glasses. Blow out the flame as it flares and the supported match will be fused to the side of the glass. You can then draw away the other glass, invert it, and ease it against the bottom of the match which is still extending horizontally from the glass to which the head is attached.

2. KNOCK IT AWAY A quarter is placed on a bare table and an empty soda bottle is stood upside down upon the coin. The trick now is to remove the quarter without touching the bottle, which must remain standing on the table.

Use a flat-bladed table knife. Bring the blade along the table and make a swift sidewise sweep, chopping the coin right out from under the bottle. Be sure to make a long follow through, so the knife will be clear as the bottle takes a tiny downward jolt and remains on the table, still balanced upside down.

3. TAKE IT AWAY Lay a dollar bill on the table; upon it, set a glass of water. Challenge anyone to remove the bill without touching the glass. This means without touching the glass

2

with *anything*, except of course the dollar bill, which is already in contact with the glass.

The trick is done with the dollar bill itself. Start rolling the bill from the near end, forming it into a compact cylinder. As your fingers approach the glass, move them to the sides of the bill so they will not touch the glass as you continue the rolling process.

The tightened center of the bill pushes the glass ahead of it, drawing the rest of the bill from beneath.

4. THE COIN GUESS This is a neat baffler with three coins, more of a "catch" than a trick, but with a surprise conclusion that everyone will appreciate.

Holding three coins in your closed hand, you jingle them and state: "I have here three coins that add up to exactly thirty-five cents, but one of them is *not* a nickel. Guess what those coins are!"

Usually all guesses will fail, because no one can figure three coins totalling thirty-five cents without a nickel among them. Finally you show the three coins; they consist of a quarter and two nickels.

Before the puzzled looks fade, point to the quarter and remind your listeners: "I said that *one* of the coins was *not* a nickel and this is the coin."

It's just a case of wording but the more boldly it is done, the better it succeeds. People naturally infer that your statement "one of them is *not* a nickel" means that none of the coins is a nickel, whereas actually you have stipulated precisely the opposite.

5. THE BILL AND THE BOTTLES The requirements for this ingenious baffler are two empty soda bottles and a dollar

3

bill or a piece of paper of equivalent size. One bottle is placed upon the table, the dollar bill is set on top of it and the other bottle is inverted upon the bill.

This requires some careful balancing, with the result that the bill is safely trapped between the mouths of the bottles. Then comes the great problem: namely, to remove the dollar bill from between the bottles without touching either bottle.

To do it, draw the dollar bill taut with one hand, being careful not to jog the bottles. Raise the other hand, extend the first two fingers and bring them down sharply and smartly upon the dollar bill, half way between the end of the bill and the bottles.

Be sure to follow this stroke through and the bill will be whisked cleanly from between the bottles, leaving them balanced mouth to mouth. To facilitate the trick, the bill can be set off center, allowing a long end for the stroke.

6. IT WON'T BURN   Of all combustible products, a cigarette paper should take top rank, as its proper function is to burn. Nevertheless, you can prove that an ordinary cigarette paper *won't* burn.

Take the cigarette paper and press it against the side of a drinking tumbler, following the curve of the glass. Keep the paper spread smooth between the thumb and forefinger of one hand while you apply a lighted match to the paper with your other hand.

The paper won't burn, because the glass absorbs the heat and thus protects it from the flame.

7. THE IMPOSSIBLE DRINK   Here is a problem to challenge great minds: How to take a drink from a bottle without removing the cork, in fact without opening the bottle at all. It's one of those things that you can really do after everyone agrees that it must be impossible.

4

All you need is the right type of bottle, the sort that has a raised bottom forming a large cavity beneath the bottle. Many wine bottles are of this type. Invert the bottle, pour in a drink from a glass, then drink it out of the bottom of the bottle. That fulfills the order of taking a drink from a bottle without opening it.

8. PEPPER AND SALT Spill some salt on the table and on the salt, sprinkle a small quantity of pepper. By that simple action you produce a dilemma, for your problem now is to remove the pepper from the salt, without touching either. Not a grain of pepper is to be left amid the salt.

The secret weapon which will accomplish this formidable task is an ordinary pocket comb. Run it through your hair to generate some electricity, then draw the comb above the mixture of salt and pepper. The pepper grains, being lighter will jump to the comb, leaving the salt clear and white.

Some of the salt will be attracted to the comb too, but that doesn't matter, as your proposition was simply to clear away the pepper.

9. COINS ON EDGE Balancing a coin on edge isn't difficult, unless your nerves are that way already. Hence you won't have too much trouble tricking your friends with this little catch.

Begin by saying that is is very difficult to stand a coin on edge, particularly a coin like a quarter. When someone says that he can do it, you respond: "All right. I'll give you a nickel for every quarter you can stand on edge!"

The more quarters he balances, the better, provided they are his own quarters. You simply pick them up and give him a nickel for each quarter, which is exactly what you promised to do.

10. DIME UNDER GLASS   This one comes from an almost-forgotten book on magic written more than a hundred years ago. On the dinner table, place a dime, over it invert a glass. Now you are to remove the dime without touching the glass, or changing its position on the table.

Take two half dollars and shove them under the edges of the glass on opposite sides, thus elevating the glass slightly without changing its position. Then scratch the table cloth in front of the glass and the dime will wangle forward and out. Remove the half dollars without touching the glass, which stays right where it was.

If you've seen this done with the half dollars already in position, you now know the complete trick. It's not an improvement; it's just that the original method has finally caught up with its half-way imitation, after a century of magical progress.

11. DROP THE MATCH   Simply a paper match, torn from a pack, but it presents a pressing problem. Holding the match a few inches above the table, you are supposed to drop it so that it will land on its side and stay there. Let people try it with paper matches and when they give up, show them how easy it is.

All you do is fix your match beforehand. Split or separate it from the bottom, well up to the head. Hold the match delicately near the bottom, pressing the split sections together. That's why it's a pressing problem, but it's solved when you drop the match. The sections will curve apart and the match will land on its spread side and stay there.

12. POKER PUZZLER   You need a pack of cards to sell this one. Bring up the question of the famous game of Poker,

6

regarding the highest hand that anyone can hold in a regulation game, without benefit of wild deuces, jokers or other variants. Someone will inform you that a Royal Flush is the highest hand in a Poker game, at which you shake your head and say: "You can't beat Four Aces with a Royal Flush."

If somebody bets he can, don't let him. It wouldn't be fair to win a bet so easily. Just pick up the pack and take out the four aces. Show them and say: "There's my hand, Four Aces. Try and beat it with a Royal Flush." Give him the pack, so he can draw out his Royal Flush, but he won't be able to do it.

Since a Royal Flush consists of the *ace*, king, queen, jack and ten of a single suit, there are none in the pack, as you have appropriated all the aces for yourself.

13. DRINK THE WATER   Set a glass of water on your outstretched right hand. Let two people grip your arm with both their hands and state that despite all their efforts to hold your arm, you can lift the glass to your mouth and drink the water.

As soon as they have grimly tightened their grip, reach out with your *left* hand, lift the glass from your right palm, carry the glass to your lips and drink the water. Very simple, when you think of it, only people seldom do.

14. TAKE IT OFF   Slide the handle of a cup along a pencil and let the cup hang from the pencil while someone holds the ends. The problem now is to remove the cup from the pencil, in full view, without breaking the cup handle. In fact, a plastic or metal cup may be used to render this impossible. Nor is the spectator to release the ends of the pencil.

It's simply a "catch" that fulfills the terms and leaves no room for argument. Just lift the cup slightly and hold it there, so that the handle no longer contacts the pencil. You have actually removed the cup from the pencil, as nobody can deny. Of course you have to put it back on the pencil again, but that's another story.

15. JUMP OVER IT Hypnotism is a wonderful thing. With just a few hypnotic passes, you can make it impossible for a person to jump over his hat when you place it on the floor. Of course you're bound to find someone who will dispute this, so the only thing is to prove it.

Take the hat and lay it in the very corner of the room. Then make your hypnotic passes and tell the victim to jump over the hat—if he can. Naturally, he can't, as there are too many walls in the way.

Incidentally, it doesn't matter whether you make those passes at the victim or his hat. It works either way.

16. BUTTON IT UP When you want to lose a friend, try this one on him. Offer to bet that he can't unbutton his vest and button it up in less than twenty seconds. If he isn't wearing a vest, make the same suggestion regarding his coat, but cut the time limit to fifteen seconds.

Accepting your challenge, your friend (which he still is up to this time) unbuttons his vest and rebuttons it, stating that he has won. You then remark that he didn't button his vest *up;* instead, he buttoned it *down*. By then the twenty seconds have passed and you have won the challenge.

17. TURN-OVER CARD A playing card is placed face down on the floor and covered with a felt hat. The magician then states that he will cause the card to turn face up without touching it.

Of course everyone expects a "catch" but there isn't any. The trick is done quite legitimately, although the demonstration reveals the method of operation.

Press down on the crown of the hat, then lift the hat with a quick sweep. The suction thus created will cause the card to fly in the air and do a complete flip, landing face up on the floor.

18. MATCH-BOX TOSS   Take an empty wooden match-box and give it a spinning toss in air, so that it lands on the table or the floor. When you do this, state that you will make the box land with its label up. That it does and practically every time, it lands the same way.

When you pass other match-boxes to people so that they can try it, they don't get the same result. Obviously, your tosses are the result of long and arduous practice, which must have taken years to reach perfection.

So it seems, but there is a trick to it. Plant a couple of coins between the drawer of the match box and the cover, at the bottom. These add weight that will make the box land label up.

19. THE LIGHTER END   Picking up a box of matches, you hold it to your head and tell which way the heads are pointing. When you push open the drawer, your guess is seen to be correct.. This might be luck, except that you promptly repeat it, with a dozen boxes if you wish, always naming the head end correctly.

There's an old joke about the head of a match being the *lighter* end. Actually it is the heavier end and with a box full of matches, those "lighters"—otherwise heads—add considerable weight. Stand each match-box on its side, lift it between thumb and finger, which press the top and bottom. Do this lightly and the box will tilt downward at one end, indicating the position of the heads.

20. TWELVE THOUSAND—AND WHAT? This is one of my favorite "Bafflers" which I have used often during radio broadcasts, working it on an entire studio audience. The process is to hand around some pencils and paper; then tell people to write the number: "Twelve thousand, twelve hundred and twelve."

Tell them not to hesitate, but to write it quickly—"Twelve thousand, twelve hundred and twelve"—a very simple number. But the faster they try to write it, the more perplexed they get. Most of them come up with 121212, which is one hundred and twenty-one thousand, two hundred and twelve, and sometimes they produce even more outlandish results.

The answer, which you finally divulge, is that there *is* no such number as twelve thousand, twelve hundred and twelve, at least not in common parlance. What you have to do is add the component numbers: 12,000, 1200, 12. That gives you 13,212 so the number they are after is actually thirteen thousand, two hundred and twelve—though your statement of the case is legitimate enough.

21. THE BALANCED COIN *The problem:* To balance a coin on edge without touching it, which would indeed seem an impossible task.

Use a large coin, preferably a half dollar, and lay it on the center of an outspread handkerchief. Take the diagonal corners of the handkerchief, draw them tightly, and lift.

The coin will be trapped in a center crease of the cloth and

10

you can easily make it stand upright, particularly by working your hands inward from the corner to shorten the crease.

22. THE DROPPING COIN Take a strip of paper about twelve inches long and one inch wide; form it into a circle and paste the ends, one slightly overlapping the other.

This paper ring is set upon the mouth of a drinking glass and on top of the paper, directly above the glass, you place a small coin, such as a dime or a penny.

Holding a pencil about a foot to the right of the balanced paper ring, you make a long hard stroke to the left, hitting the paper ring which is knocked away. The coin drops straight down and plunks into the glass.

A neat little stunt, everyone agrees, but it shouldn't be too difficult to do. That being the case, you invite your friends to try it. They knock away the paper loop, as you did, but the coin goes flying with it. Only the master (that's you!) can make the coin drop in the glass.

There's a reason, of course. That long sweep of the pencil, from the right, is just so much fakery. As you swing, you purposely miss the outside of the loop (on the right) and catch the inside of the loop, at the left. Your follow through literally hooks the paper ring and whips it out from beneath the coin which immediately drops straight down.

This happens so fast that observers think you have knocked away the loop instead of hooking it, so when they try the trick they invariably do it the wrong way.

23. SEEING THINGS Strictly an optical illusion, but a very unusual one. Hold your hands on a level with your eyes, at slightly less than arm's length. Then put the fingers of your forefingers together and look at them with a far-away stare.

11

Very shortly a little sausage will appear between the tips of the fingers, but that is only the beginning. While you watch the sausage, draw your fingers apart a few inches, very slowly. The sausage will round itself into a little ball that will remain suspended in mid-air between your magnetic finger-tips.

24. YOUR CHOICE   Certain cigarette packs have the words CHOICE QUALITY printed in capital letters along the side. Open the outer cellophane wrapping of such a pack and slide it so that it covers only one of those words, not the other.

Turn the pack so the words are upside down and let someone look at the printing in a mirror. To his surprise, the word CHOICE will appear exactly as it should, while the word QUALITY is reversed in the mirror.

You explain this on the influence of the cellophane, but the real reason is that the letters in CHOICE when inverted and reversed, appear as normal. Instead of the mirror, you can look at the inverted words through a transparent swizzle stick and the result will be the same.

25. FULL AND EMPTY   Five small glasses are set in a row. The three in the center are filled with water; the end glasses are empty. The proposition is to move those glasses so that they are alternately empty and full, or as you can phrase it: "I want to rearrange these glasses so that every full one is next to an empty." Then you add that this must be done in the least number of moves and that every time you touch a glass it constitutes a move.

If the glasses are set rather well apart, two moves would appear the logical answer. All anyone has to do is move the two empties from the ends in between a pair of full glasses. But you can beat that by moving only *one* glass.

Just pick up the middle glass, drink the water, and put the glass back where you found it. Every full glass is now next to an empty, the difference being that there are only two full glasses instead of three.

26. THE BALANCED DICE Take a pair of dice and spin one on its corner, like a top. State that it is easy enough for a die to remain upright while spinning, but to balance it while standing still is even simpler. You can do it with either of the dice, using nothing but the dice.

They want to see it, so you show them. Set one of the dice on the table with its one-spot up. Set the corner of the other in the depressed spot and it will balance there without any difficulty.

27. THREE COIN SHIFT Place three coins in a row so that their edges touch. The two coins at the left are heads up, the one at the right is tails up. The object is to move the tail-up coin to the center place.

But in doing this, there are limiting conditions. The coin on the left can be moved, but *not* touched; the coin in the center can be touched but *not* moved. This turns the whole enterprise into quite a problem.

Here is the method: Place your left forefinger firmly on the center coin. Move the coin on the right with your right forefinger, taking it a few inches to the right. Then sweep it hard to the left, striking the side of the center coin.

The center coin does not move, but the force of the blow will carry through and knock away the coin on the left. This leaves a space between the head-up coins into which you triumphantly slide the tail-up coin.

28. ODD IS EVEN A neat "catch" with figures. State that you can write five odd figures that will add up to exactly twenty. This sounds impossible, because an odd number of odd numbers will always add up to an odd total.

But you are speaking of *figures,* not numbers. Those that you use are 1, 1, 1, 1 and 7. When you add them up, you do it thus:

$$
\begin{array}{r}
17 \\
1 \\
1 \\
1 \\
\hline
20
\end{array}
$$

29. COINS AND GLASS This trick seems impossible of accomplishment, and one may require some practice to do it correctly—but the appearance of difficulty will add to its value.

Place two coins on the opposite edges of a water glass, and ask the spectator to remove both coins by the use of the thumb and one finger of the same hand. They must be removed at the same time—the thumb touching one coin—the finger the other —and they must not be allowed to drop on the table.

With these exacting conditions, no one thinks it can be done, but here is the method: Place the thumb on one coin and the finger on the other. Tilt them so that they slant outwards, pressing to keep them from falling—which brings the coins to the sides of the glass, instead of the upper edge. Drawing them downward and slowly toward yourself, you suddenly bring your finger and thumb together and the coins snap together, free of the glass.

With a bit of practice, this can be done quickly and easily and is very rewarding as the solution of a perplexing problem.

30. A SMOKE TRICK This trick is contrary to nature in that smoke rises *up*ward—and you can demonstrate that it will go *down*ward.

Use the cellophane wrapper from a cigar, which is a perfect tube. Hold it vertically and ignite the top. Smoke will appear, but instead of rising, it will descend into the transparent wrapper, under the flame.

31. DROP THE CARDS This "Baffler" can be turned into a very provoking problem until you finally prove that it really can be done. The problem is to hold some playing cards shoulder high and drop them one by one into a hat that is waiting, brim up, on the floor directly beneath.

Each card is pointed downward and should go straight into the hat, but somewhere during the trip, the air will catch it and send it scooting away from its target. You can help people aim their cards, suggest they drop them with the side pointing downward, but it is all no use.

Then comes your turn. Simply hold each card flat and let it drop level. The cards will waver as they drop but will settle squarely into the hat. You float them home, that's all.

32. KNOTTING A CIGARETTE Tying a knot in a cigarette sounds like an impossibility, but it can be accomplished, and quite legitimately.

Take the cellophane wrapping from a pack of cigarettes; spread it flat and place the cigarette in the center, running the long way in relation to the cellophane.

Now roll the cigarette tightly in the cellophane which will thus form a long tube containing the cigarette. Next tie the cellophane in a knot, cigarette and all. You will have to force the cigarette into the knot, but the cellophane will protect it

15

and eventually the cigarette will be seen, actually tied, within its transparent wrapping.

When untied, the cigarette can be straightened out and shown undamaged, still in condition to be smoked. A long cigarette is preferable for the trick as it allows more leeway in forming the knot.

33. THE JUMPING FLAME The magician lights two matches. He blows one out and holds it just beneath the flame of the other. Immediately the lower match lights itself.

To work this trick successfully, hold the lighted match above the unlighted one immediately after the latter has been blown out. A tiny smoke stream will rise from the extinguished match. The flame of the upper match catches this stream, follows it down and relights the lower match almost instantly.

Chapter 2

TABLE TRICKS

TABLE TRICKS ARE THE NATURAL OUTGROWTH OF IM-
promptu stunts and problems; therefore almost every magician
is called upon to perform them at times. This is particularly
true with the magician who makes magic a social pastime, as
his friends will always be calling upon him to display his wares
as an after-dinner recreation.

Therefore, tricks of this type should be among the first that
anyone learns. They include tricks that are specially suited
for close range while seated at a table and they also consist of
tricks that can be done with objects commonly found on a
table.

Being essentially a form of impromptu magic, such tricks
should preferably be the sort that need no special equipment.
Hence the tricks that compose this chapter have been kept
within that range. Most of them can be quickly acquired by
beginners; nevertheless, all tricks improve with practice, so it
should not be neglected.

In other chapters, the reader will find more tricks that are
adaptable to the restrictions of table performance, but which
have been included in broader categories. These can be used

as added features by performers who wish to specialize in table magic.

1. FLOATING SUGAR As an impromptu trick for the dinner table, this can be developed into quite a mystery. Taking a flat lump of sugar, the magician sets it in a cup of coffee and it floats there until he commands it to sink.

Then, as if under genuine magic control, the lump gradually goes from sight and the magician stirs his coffee as though nothing had happened. Of course if there are skeptics present —and usually there are—they will want to stir the coffee too and see if they can find a clue. But all they will discover is sugar.

That's all there is to the trick: Sugar. But there is more of it than people suppose. Before showing the trick, the magician secretly drops a lump of sugar into the coffee, but does this very carefully so the lump remains standing on its end, below the surface of the liquid.

Picking up another lump of sugar, the wizard calls attention to it and places it in the cup, broad side down, stating he will make it float. In doing this he sets it neatly on the hidden lump; hence the visible lump appears to be floating on the surface.

Meanwhile the hidden lump is melting, so as soon as the visible lump begins to wabble, the magician commands it to sink, which it promptly does. It is preferable to have cream in the coffee to make certain that the upright lump will not be seen.

2. THE STRONG STRAW Passing several drinking straws among the spectators, the magician takes one and slides the handle of a cup over it. Then, carefully lifting the ends of the straw, he causes it to support the hanging cup.

Other people who try the trick find that they lack the necessary power over straws, for in their case the weight of the cup bends the straw and causes it to collapse.

The difference is this: in the straw that he uses, the magician has previously inserted a length of wire, not quite as long as the straw. In gripping the ends of the straw he holds the wire also and it is what supports the weight.

Performed at the dinner table, this trick is particularly effective, since while the spectators are failing with their straws, the magician can tilt his straw over the table edge and release the wire, which will fall to the floor.

Then the magician can hand his straw to someone else who wants to try the trick, only to prove that the magician's straw is quite as vulnerable as the rest, when used by someone who lacks the magic influence.

3. FIND THE MATCHES The magician shows three match boxes—two are empty, one is filled with matches. He shakes the full box and the matches rattle. He moves the match boxes about the table, shakes one empty one and then the other. People are asked to pick the full match box, which they do.

Repeating the procedure, the magician leaves two match boxes on the table and drops the third in his pocket. Again, the telltale rattle has enabled the spectators to pick the full box. It is the one that went into the magician's pocket.

Bringing out the full box, the magician repeats the movement of the boxes. This time, the spectators pick the wrong box. They think that an empty one is the full one. Time and again, the magician baffles them. Always, the full box shows up at an unexpected spot.

Four match boxes are used. At the beginning, you have three on the table: a full box and two empties. In your pocket you have another full box, but it differs slightly from the one on the table.

The box in your pocket must be so fully packed with matches that none of them will rattle. Opened, it shows as a full box of matches. Closed, it will make no noise when you shake it.

Ask the spectators to pick the full box. They do so without difficulty. You open the full box, show the matches and shake it when you close it. Mix the match boxes more rapidly this time, shaking one empty, then the other. Quickly carry the full box to your pocket.

Ask where the full box is. People say: "In your pocket." Dropping the box in your pocket, you bring out the other full box, which is tightly packed. Open it and show it full of matches. Close it and place it with the empties.

This time, you *do not* shake the full box until after you have quickly mixed the boxes on the table. The spectators lose track of the full one. Pick up an empty, shake it violently. Pick up the full box and shake it just as hard. The packed matches prevent it from rattling. The spectators think that the third, unshaken box must be the full one.

Mix the boxes gingerly, but at fair speed, as though trying to prevent a rattle. Spectators follow the box that you did not shake. They call it the full one. Open that box and show it empty. Show the full box elsewhere.

Repeat this routine, never shaking the full box while the spectators know which one it is. After you have fooled them three or four times, dump the matches from the full box to show that it is an ordinary one.

4. FIVE COIN TWISTER   Five coins are laid on the table—three pennies and two dimes. They are arranged in alternating order, so that no two coins of the same denomination come side by side.

The problem is to move the coins two at a time, to new positions. Each move must be made with two coins that are side by side, and eleven cents must be shifted with each move. That is, a penny and a dime must figure in each action. At the end of four moves, pennies and dimes are to form separate groups.

The performer accomplishes this swiftly and smoothly, with four simple moves. It looks easy, but when spectators attempt the trick, they bungle. Even when the moves are repeated, the fail to catch the system.

The moves follow a definite rule. On every move except the third, have a dime on the *left* of the pair you move. On the third move, a *penny* must be on the left. Certain moves are obvious if you follow this system—but there are other points to be remembered. Practice the moves as follows.

First Move: Move either dime and the penny to the right of it. Slide the pair to the left end of the line, but leave a space of about two inches between that pair and the penny which marks the original left end of the line.

Second Move: Move the other dime and the penny to the right of it. Carry them to the left of the first pair.

Third Move: Only one dime has a penny to the left of it. Move that dime and the penny on its left. Carry them *between* the two remaining pennies.

Fourth Move: Take the dime and penny which are on the right end of the line. Move them in between the other dime and two pennies.

The final arrangement is thus obtained. The coins are segregated: two dimes at the left, three pennies at the right.

5. ROLLING THE BILLS The magician places a five dollar bill upon the table, pointing it away from him at an angle to the left. He lays a one dollar bill upon the five, but points the one dollar bill at right angles to the five, so that only the inner end of the five is covered by the inner end of the one.

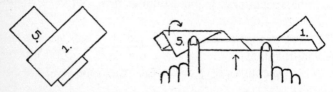

The bills thus form a "V", with the point toward the magician. Thereupon, the magician starts rolling the bills together, starting at the point and rolling them tightly *away* from him. He unrolls the bills to show the one on top. He rolls them again and lets a person place a finger upon the one.

The magician places his left forefinger upon the projecting corner of the five and unrolls the bills with his right hand. To the utter amazement of all viewers, the five dollar bill is *above* the one dollar bill.

The shift comes when the bills are almost completely rolled. Have your hands on the rolled centers. Point to the corner of the one dollar bill with your right hand and ask a spectator to place his finger upon it.

Your left hand is almost covering the last corner of the five dollar bill. Simply slide your left hand a few inches forward, pressing as you do so. With this movement, you slide the rolled up portion of the five so that its projecting corner comes underneath and flips over the top. This shift does the trick.

22

The movement is covered by the left hand, and the left forefinger must immediately press the corner of the five dollar bill against the table, while the right hand returns to the rolled up center. When the right hand unrolls the held bills, the five-spot will be on top.

6. MAGNETIZED KNIFE   Holding a table knife in his hands, the magician folds his fingers and extends their backs toward the spectators. The table knife rests between the palms of his hands—his thumbs hold it in position.

The hands are raised to the vertical—they are clasped across in front of the magician's body. The knife is upright. Part of it projects above the hands, part below. The magician announces that the knife is magnetized.

People ridicule this theory, because the magician's thumbs are out of sight and could obviously be holding the knife in its position. The magician volunteers to show his thumbs; he raises one, lowers it. He repeats the maneuver with the other thumb. The spectators laugh, because they think that the magician is merely transferring the burden from one thumb to the other.

The laugh ends when the magician raises both thumbs. The knife does not fall. It remains behind his fingers, invisibly supported. It stays there until he pulls his hands apart—then the knife drops to the table and is immediately given for examination.

This trick is easily accomplished, and its secret is quite elusive. It depends upon the middle finger of the right hand. When you fold your hands, you do not do so in the ordinary fashion. Instead, you slide your fingers together, end to end.

The knife should be lying on the left palm. As you bring the right hand toward the left, bend the right second finger inward.

Slide the right forefinger between the first and second fingers of the left hand. The third finger of the right hand goes between the second and third of the left. The little finger of the right hand goes between the third and the little finger of the left.

When you raise the backs of the hands toward the spectators, they see only *seven* fingers instead of eight. The position of the fingers is so natural that they never think of counting the fingers. They are more interested in your thumbs, which are out of sight in the palms of your hands.

The middle finger of your right hand is on the inner side of the knife. Its pressure actually holds the knife in place. The thumbs merely appear to hold the knife. After you have kept up the bluff for a while, extend the thumb straight upward. The knife will still adhere, thanks to the support of the hidden finger.

Retain this final position just long enough to convince the spectators that the knife is actually adhering to the hands without support. Move the hands back and forth, toward the spectators and away from them. Do this deliberately, tilting the hands slightly forward and backward. Ten seconds should be about the limit of this demonstration. At the end of that period, pull the hands apart and let the knife fall.

7. BLACKSTONE'S PAPER BALL TRICK Three little paper pellets are lying on the table. Two of them are dropped in the left hand. The third is thrown away, but when the left hand is opened, out roll the three paper balls.

Time and again the trick is repeated. Yet the three paper balls constantly return to the left hand. When the trick is finished with some of the variations that will be given, the spectators are unanimous in declaring it one of the most perplexing mysteries they have ever witnessed.

A fourth paper ball is used, and it is concealed between the tips of the first and second fingers of the right hand. It is placed there with the aid of the thumb, which holds it against the second finger until the forefinger is ready to take its place.

With the extra ball in position, pick up the first paper ball between the thumb and the tip of the forefinger. You can show the inside of your hand as you do so, for the thumb hides the extra ball. Drop the first paper ball in the left hand.

Repeat the movement with the second ball, but in dropping it in the hand, let the extra ball go with it, immediately closing the left hand.

Spread the fingers of the right hand, and pick up the third ball between the thumb and second finger. Pretend to throw it away, but clip it between your finger tips. Roll the three paper balls from the left hand, and you are ready to start again.

By way of variation, reach under the table and pretend to knock the third paper ball up through.

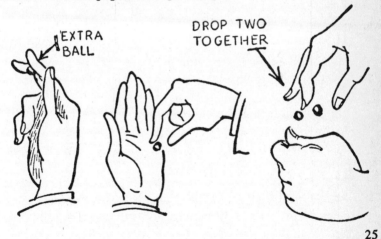

EXTRA BALL

DROP TWO TOGETHER

Another neat effect is to drop the third ball in the pocket—apparently. Always retain it in the right hand.

By way of variation, cup the left hand, and in dropping the first paper ball, let the extra ball go in. This gives you unusual freedom with the second ball, which follows. Then throw the third away. The three will be in the left hand.

The big surprise is the introduction of some other object, such as a coin or a lump of sugar. Drop the third ball in the pocket, and while rolling out three from the left hand, obtain the other article. Then place two balls in the left hand, without showing the right empty, and let the large object drop in also. Pretend to throw the third ball away, and the coin or lump of sugar will roll from the left hand instead.

Place the two balls in the left hand, and let the extra one fall with them. Put the large object in your pocket, and the three balls again appear in the left hand.

Now comes a vanish of the three paper balls. Put them one by one into the left hand (apparently), but retain each in the right hand, between the fingers. When you pocket the third ball, drop all three in your pocket; and show your left hand empty.

With a little preparation you can add some good effects to the Paper Ball Trick. Take some ordinary pins and push them through the cloth under your vest, so that the points are downward. Impale three paper balls on each pin.

After vanishing the paper balls, show the left hand empty, then extend the right hand and show it empty too. At the same time, the left hand goes to the vest and draws off three paper balls.

Everyone wonders where the balls have gone, and when you extend your left hand, they roll on the table again. During the surprise, your right hand captures three from one of the pin points, then the left hand drops the three paper balls in the pocket on the left side, and the right hand rolls the balls on the table.

By retaining one ball in the left hand, you can hold it cupped; then the right hand drops two in the left and throws the third away—the three appear in the left. You are back at the beginning again—and at a later period you can get three more from your vest to conclude the trick.

Of course the routine should not be overdone. At the same time it is one of those tricks that gets better as it progresses—and it should be adapted to the occasion. When to do a trick and how long to do it is something that must be learned by experience.

8. TOPSY TURVY MATCH PACK All you need is an empty paper match pack. You bend this inward, so that it

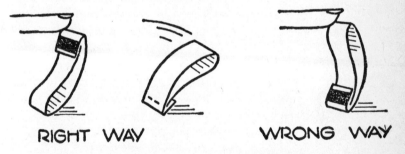

RIGHT WAY   WRONG WAY

forms a curve, and set it upright on the table, holding it balanced there with your finger. At the word "Go!," you release the pack and it promptly turns a somersault. That done, you give the match pack to some other person and ask him to try it. But it just won't "go" when he gives the command, though it works for you every time.

27

The secret is this: When you set the match pack on the table, you must balance it *upside down.* When you release it, the match pack will somersault along its outward curve. But when you give it to another person, hand him the pack *right side up.* When he attempts the trick it won't work, because the weight of the striking surface is all at the bottom.

9. THE BALANCED NAPKIN Here's a surprising trick with a paper napkin. You simply raise it upright, from one diagonal corner to the other and it remains in that position as though magnetized. With a little practice you can make the trick even more wonderful by balancing the standing napkin on your finger tip. Other people try it, but fail. What is your strange power over paper napkins?

The Answer: Before you start the demonstration, secretly draw the napkin taut from opposite diagonal corners. Don't draw too hard or you will tear the napkin, and should you tear it, use another. Nevertheless, be sure to apply a firm pull. This stretches the fibres in the paper and stiffens them so that the napkin can be balanced on either of those corners.

10. X-RAY SIGHT This is a very effective trick for the dinner table, inasmuch as several persons can participate. Give the people a coin and state that it has an X-ray quality. While your back is turned, one person is to take the coin in his hand and hold it to his head, thus producing the necessary mental vibration.

After that, all the persons place their hands along the table with their fists closed. Moving your finger from hand to hand, you finally point out the one that contains the coin. The trick may be repeated with the same success.

Here is the secret: The hand that was raised will become

whiter than the others because the blood leaves it while the person holds his hand to his head. Just look for the hand that doesn't match it's mate and you will have the hand that contains the coin.

Chapter 3

CARD SLEIGHTS

HERE THE READER WILL FIND USEFUL METHODS IN CARD handling that he can apply constantly in card tricks. The first of these are false shuffles and false cuts—always of value.

The other sleights in this section have been included because they are of use in certain tricks which could not otherwise be performed successfully. With the present trend of card magic, there is no purpose in utilizing all sorts of manipulations. Nevertheless, certain tricks require the introduction of some bit of skill.

The reader should familiarize himself with all of the methods given in this section so he can refer to them as he proceeds. If he likes a particular trick that depends upon the "glide" or the "palm," he can then spend time in practicing the sleight.

Any feats of skill with cards are useful, as they represent a definite step in the smooth handling of cards. At the same time, the old idea of practicing sleights that had no practical use is something which can scarcely be recommended. The sleights in this section were placed there after the major portion of the book had been written and they were found to be necessary for reference in certain tricks.

1. FALSE SHUFFLES False shuffles are useful in connection with many card tricks. Through their aid, the performer can keep a card on the top or bottom of the pack; or can retain the entire deck in its regular order.

Such shuffles are not difficult to learn, although they should be practiced frequently. They must simulate genuine shuffles; therefore, some of the best false shuffles are patterned directly after ordinary ways of shuffling the pack.

In Blackstone's "Modern Card Tricks and Secrets of Magic," we outlined a false shuffling system for use with the "Card Control." Other methods of false shuffling are given here, with a few references to the system described in the previous book. There is no reason why any performer should attempt to utilize a wide variety of false shuffles. The shuffle is simply used to mix the cards—and it is natural for a person to shuffle the cards in one way. The magician, therefore, is apt to bring suspicion upon himself if he shuffles differently each time he handles the cards.

Most persons, however, utilize both the dovetail shuffle and the overhand shuffle, as well as cuts, when they are mixing the cards. Therefore we are giving practical methods of false shuffling both dovetail and overhand, with a section on false cuts in addition.

2. DOVETAIL FALSE SHUFFLES In the dovetail shuffle, the executor simply divides the pack into two portions and riffles the ends, allowing the two sections of the pack to interweave. In doing this, it is best to let the inner corners of the packets run together, under control of the thumbs.

In many tricks, the magician desires to keep the top card in its position; in others, he may wish to keep the bottom card in position. This is easy with the dovetail shuffle—in fact it is so natural that there is virtually no falsity about the shuffle.

To keep the top card in position, simply dovetail in the usual fashion, but be sure to retain the top card until after all others have fallen. By this method, one can keep a dozen cards or more on top of the pack. Presuming that the upper portion of the pack is taken in the right hand, it is desirable that the upper portion should be slightly larger than the lower. By riffling the lower portion more rapidly than the upper, the left hand finishes with its cards while those in the right are still being riffled. The top cards remain on top.

To retain the bottom cards in position, they are simply allowed to fall first. In this case, the left hand, with the bottom heap, runs ahead of the right, dropping a number of cards before the right hand begins its release.

Retaining cards on both top and bottom is simplicity with the dovetail shuffle. Dividing the pack into two equal heaps, the left hand lets the lower cards go first; then the right hand follows and when the left hand packet is exhausted, the right hand is still riffling cards.

The ordinary false shuffle by the dovetail method is scarcely more than an imperfect shuffle which the performer turns to his own advantage. Yet the spectators, unsuspecting of his purpose, have no idea that he is deliberately controlling the cards.

3. COMPLETE PACK CONTROL (*With the Dovetail*)

The apparent shuffling of the pack without disturbing the arrangement of a single card may be accomplished with the dovetail shuffle. This is a real false shuffle. It will require considerable practice, in order to render it deceptive.

The right hand heap represents the upper portion of the pack. It should contain fewer cards than the left hand heap.

Cards are riffled first from the left hand, giving that packet a start. Following, the right hand ends with some of its cards on top of the pack.

Up to this point the shuffle is genuine. The spectators are allowed to see that the inner corners of the pack are actually dovetailed. Only the very corners are interlaced, however. As though to complete the shuffle, the performer swings his fingers together. As he does so, he bends the outer end of the right portion upward. The fingers come together and by a slight drawing of the thumbs, the interwoven corners of the pack are separated.

The upward bend of the outer corner of the right heap enables it to slide up on top of the left heap and thus the hands come together, simulating exactly the completion of an ordinary dovetail shuffle. The fingers prevent anyone from observing that the shuffle is not bona fide.

This shuffle should be practiced until it is natural. It reaches a point where just the slightest twist enables the magician to change a genuine shuffle into a false one. By using this mode of shuffling regularly, he can make the movement highly convincing, no matter how closely the observers may happen to be watching.

4. OVERHAND FALSE SHUFFLE (*To Control Bottom Cards*) In the simplest and most natural form of the overhand shuffle, the shuffler holds the deck in his left hand and peels off several cards with the thumb. The remainder of the pack is brought down by the right hand and more cards are peeled off. This is continued until all the cards have been shuffled off.

To control bottom cards during a normal overhand shuffle, the performer simply grips them with the tips of his left

33

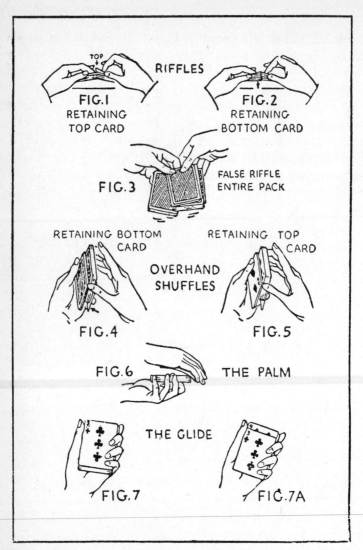

RIFFLES

FIG.1
RETAINING
TOP CARD

FIG.2
RETAINING
BOTTOM CARD

FIG.3

FALSE RIFFLE
ENTIRE PACK

RETAINING BOTTOM
CARD

RETAINING TOP
CARD

OVERHAND
SHUFFLES

FIG.4

FIG.5

FIG.6

THE PALM

THE GLIDE

FIG.7

FIG.7A

The diagrams show the correct positions for various preliminary sleights explained in this chapter.

fingers when the left thumb peels off the first layer of cards. Result: the bottom cards are retained beneath the top ones. The rest of the pack is shuffled on top and the bottom cards are not disturbed.

By this method the performer can control a single bottom card and also bring a card from the top to go with it. He does this by peeling away the lone top card and shuffling the rest of the pack on it. He retains the bottom card when he draws down the top one. This shuffle is executed with the left side toward the audience.

5. OVERHAND FALSE SHUFFLE (*To Control Top Cards*) In this false shuffle, the performer stands with his right side toward the audience and holds the pack in his left hand. The top of the pack is against the fingers of the left hand.

In shuffling, the pack is lifted by the right hand. The left thumb peels off a few of the bottom cards, while the left fingers retain some of the top ones. The pack is brought toward the left thumb, which peels away cards and adds them to the bottom of the cluster held in the left hand. This is continued until the right hand has shuffled away all its cards.

By this method, a bottom card may be made to join a single card at the top. Simply peel away a top card and a bottom card together, clipping them and shuffling the pack upon the bottom card.

6. TOP AND BOTTOM SHUFFLE Assuming that the magician has two cards on the top of the pack and wishes to transfer one to the bottom, he does as follows: Holding the pack in the left hand, with thumb on the bottom, he peels a

35

few cards from the bottom while the left fingers draw down one top card. He then shuffles away until only one card is left in the right hand. That card drops on the bottom of the pack. One of the top cards is still on top; the other on the bottom.

Presuming that one of two bottom cards is to go to the top while the other remains on the bottom, the magician holds the pack in his left hand with thumb on top. He peels off some top cards and draws a single bottom card beneath them. He then shuffles the pack from the right hand until only one card is left. It goes on top. Thus one bottom card is on top; the other remains on the bottom.

7. OVERHAND SHUFFLE WITH COMPLETE PACK

This is the method whereby none of the cards are disturbed during an overhand shuffle. Hold the pack in the left hand with the thumb on top. Peel off about a dozen cards with the left thumb. Bring the pack down on top of those cards and remove no cards whatever—although the motion makes it appear that you do.

Now bring the pack beneath the left hand cards and peel off some with the left thumb. Once more come on top with the right hand but leave none. Go beneath and leave some. Continue thus as though you were leaving cards on both top and bottom. Actually you are leaving them on the bottom only. In this way the entire pack is shuffled off—right back to its original condition, without a single card being disturbed.

This shuffle naturally keeps top and bottom cards in position, so it can be used for that purpose as well as for an entire deck shuffle.

8. FALSE CUTS
A false cut serves the same purpose as the false shuffle—an apparent mixing of the pack without the

mixing taking place. The usual false cut is designed to preserve the entire arrangement of the pack.

It is a simple fact that a single cut does not disturb the order of the cards, even though it does change the position of the top card. Therefore false cuts are designed to appear more thorough than a simple cut but to do no more than cut the card once.

Many of the tricks in this book involve selected cards that are on the top of the pack or the bottom; therefore the false cuts have been specially arranged so that they do not make any change at all. Despite their appearance, they leave the pack exactly as it was before the cuts were made.

Therefore these cuts, when learned, can be applied in any trick. The card conjuror may at any time give the pack a series of cuts and be sure that he is not injuring his chances of doing the trick successfully.

Many magicians neglect false cuts. This is a mistake. In all legerdemain with cards—particularly when tricks are performed at close range—false cuts add that degree of emphasis that makes the magician's work seem amazing. Furthermore, false cuts can be learned easily and done with great rapidity —even by the beginner.

9. SIMPLE FALSE CUT (*With Three Heaps*) Lay the pack on the table. Lift off about two-thirds of the cards and lay this portion six inches to the right. Lift off half of this portion and place it in the center. This makes three piles.

Put the right pile on the left. Put the center pile on top. This brings the pack back to its original position. The following table shows the piles as they are made:

1	3	2
(Bottom)	(Top)	(Middle)

2 goes on 1 and 3 goes on 2. The pack is unchanged. This is ordinarily done with one hand. With two hands, form the piles with the right hand only. Then reach across with the left and pick up heap 2, dropping it on heap 1. The right hand immediately picks up 3 and puts it on 1 and 2.

10. ANOTHER FALSE CUT (*With Four Heaps*) Lay
the pack on the table and lift off most of the cards, leaving a small heap. Drop a dozen more from the bottom, to the right of the first pile. Drop a dozen more below the first pile and put the remainder at the right. Thus:

<table>
<tr><td>1
(Bottom)</td><td>2
(Lower Middle)</td></tr>
<tr><td>3
(Upper Middle)</td><td>4
(Top)</td></tr>
</table>

Gathering: Place 3 on 2; put 4 on 2 and 3. Lay all on 1. With two hands, the left hand picks up 3, dropping it on 2; the right hand picks up 4, gathers 2 and 3 beneath it and transfers all to the top of 1.

11. SPECIAL FALSE CUT (*With Five Heaps*) This
time four heaps are formed about the pack as a center, making five heaps in all. The mode of cutting is different at the start. A few cards are lifted from the pack and laid at the upper left corner of an imaginary square. Some more are taken from the pack and put at the upper right corner. Another group from the pack is placed at the lower left; a fourth group at the lower right.

This is the arrangement:

1		2
(Top)		(Second)
	*	
	(Pack)	
3		4
(Third)		(Fourth)

Gathering: Drop 2 on 3. Drop 1 on 2 and 3. Drop 4 on pack. Place 1, 2, 3 on 4 and pack.

With two hands, the left drops 1, the right 2, the left 3, the right 4. Picking up; right places 2 on 3; left puts 1 on 2; right places 4 on pack; left puts 1, 2, 3 on 4 and pack.

12. SHUFFLE CUT This cut has the appearance of a shuffle and certainly gives the impression of a mixing of the cards. It may be performed either with the cards on the table or with the cards held by the hands alone.

The hands hold the ends of the pack. Fingers are at the far side; thumbs at the near side. The right hand draws off cards from the bottom, pulling them away between the thumb and forefinger alone. Moving above the pack, carrying its heap, the right hand grasps some of the top cards between the tip of the thumb and the second finger.

These are drawn off to the right also—the position enables the right hand to keep the two groups separated. The left hand now holds a group of cards—those which constitute the center portion of the pack.

The left hand comes above and places its cards upon the upper group held by the right hand. The left draws away both groups as one. The right hand then lays its only remaining group upon the cards that are in the left hand.

39

With a little practice, this procedure becomes simple. Learn to do it rapidly and it is very effective. It can be repeated time and again, for it brings the pack back to the starting point. No change whatever in the order of the cards.

SHUFFLE CUT

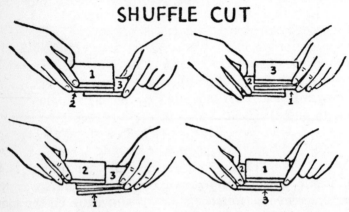

The positions of the pack during the stages of the Shuffle Cut. 1 shows the original top section; 2 the center; 3 the bottom.

13. FALSE CUT SHIFT In this method of locating a chosen card, a false cut serves the purpose of a pass. The cut is very similar to the "Shuffle Cut" elsewhere described. It is given here in detail and the reader will note the similarity.

The pack is held between the tips of thumbs and fingers. The right hand is near one end of the pack; the left near the other.

The right hand draws off the lower half of the pack between the thumb and forefinger, inviting the return of the selected card, which is placed on the lower half of the pack.

The right hand then moves above the pack and draws off the upper portion between its thumb and second finger—be-

40

low the portion already held. These sections of the pack are kept separate.

Left hand is now holding the center portion of the pack between thumb and forefinger. It comes above and with thumb and second finger draws off the upper of the two groups held by the right hand. It keeps its groups separated.

The right hand drops its one remaining group of cards upon the upper group held by the left hand and pulls away both groups as one. This leaves the left hand with its lower, single group, which it drops upon the cards in the right hand.

This puts the selected card on top of the pack, in spite of the confusing shuffle cut.

14. THE REVOLVING PASS The sleight known as the "pass" is nothing more than an invisible cut used by the magician to transpose two portions of the pack. It was for many years the recognized method of bringing a chosen card to the top of the pack.

REVOLVING PASS

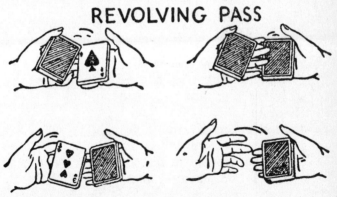

The upper half of the pack is dropped face up on the right fingers. Note how the left fingers flip it over. The lower diagrams show the other half of the pack following.

The difficulty of learning the "pass" is out of proportion to the value of the sleight, so far as the average card performer is concerned. With all the modern card detections and locations that have been devised, the "pass" is necessary only on rare occasions.

There are various forms of the "pass"—and the really good ones are hard to learn. But there are also certain "false passes" which accomplish the same purpose. The one we are about to describe is easy to do and is, at the same time, deceptive. It would not be a good sleight to use repeatedly; but it is excellent when performed occasionally.

It is included in this book so that the reader may have it available when the "pass" is actually required in any particular trick, unless he happens to be familiar with some other form of the "pass" which he finds suited to his purpose.

Hold the pack in the left hand, thumb on top, fingers beneath. The little finger is inserted in the pack at the lower right corner, holding the two portions of the pack separated. Thus, if a chosen card has been replaced in the pack, that card is just beneath the tip of the left little finger.

The right hand approaches the left. The left hand tilts toward it and lets the upper portion of the pack fall face up upon the tips of the right fingers. The left side of the portion is resting on the tips of the left fingers also (with the exception of the left little finger, which, with the left thumb, holds the lower half of the pack).

Now the left fingers give the upper portion an added flip, causing it to fall face downward in the palm of the right hand.

The right thumb now gives the bottom portion a flip from beneath so that it drops upon the finger tips of both hands, face up—just as the first heap did. Again the left fingers flip, turning this heap over. It lands upon the upper portion, in the right hand.

42

The procedure requires four movements. Each half of the pack, in turn, does a complete revolution. The upshot is that the lower heap is on top of the upper heap. The "pass" has been accomplished.

The effect is highly deceptive. There is no attempt to conceal the motion. On the contrary, it should be done boldly, in full view. It appears to be a fancy action like a riffle—a bit of jugglery that adds to the trick and seems a display of skill. It has a peculiar effect, no one realizing that it actually cuts the pack.

In using this revolving pass, the performer should first square up the pack at the front, so no one will notice the little finger of the left hand, inserted at the inner end of the pack. Then the right hand riffles the outer end of the pack, to indicate that all is fair. Immediately after the riffle comes the revolving pass.

There is no great skill needed; but the move should be practiced until the four motions blend into one, making a very pretty continuous effect. It is quite possible to throw the cards from hand to hand, letting each portion revolve as it goes from left to right. This is also a pretty effect.

The important point to remember is that the movement is actually used to transpose the sections of the pack; and it serves that purpose admirably. By using fancy cuts and riffles in other tricks, the magician can lead his observers to expect little flourishes that have no particular bearing on the trick; and when he uses the revolving pass, they will be taken entirely unaware.

15. THE PALM   One of the most useful of all card sleights is the "palm" by which a card is removed from the pack and secretly retained in the right hand. Sometimes two or more cards may be retained in this manner.

The simplest palm for a single card is the following. Hold the pack in the left hand, flat and back upward. Place the right forefinger against the outer left corner of the pack. The joint of the finger should touch the corner of the card.

The right fingers are all together. Lined in this fashion, they move forward, taking the card with them. The hand closes slightly and the fingers point downward as they go along, so that the end of the pack presses against the end of the card and it is forced tightly into the right hand.

The hand should be kept in a half-closed position, retaining the palmed card. This method enables the hand to get a firm hold on the card. The pressure should be light at first, however, so that only one card will follow the right hand.

To palm one card or more—a required number—the left thumb first pushes the cards to the right side of the pack. As the right hand covers the pack, as though to square the cards, the second finger of the left hand pushes upward from beneath and forces the cards into the right palm. This must be done neatly, to make sure that the cards are well hidden in the right hand.

16. THE GLIDE The "glide" is a very old sleight—but a very useful one and a very easy one. It was first described many years ago and it served its purposes then; however, newer tricks have utilized this sleight and it is because of this that we recommend the method to the reader.

The "glide" is actually a "second deal" in which the cards are drawn from the bottom of the pack instead of the top. It is of use only to magicians and it takes the place of a card "change."

There are two methods for the "glide." The first is the neater; the second the easier.

First Method: Hold the pack in the left hand, the thumb at the right side, the fingers curled beneath, at the left. The bulk of the hand is above the pack, which is face down. Show the bottom card by tilting up the pack. Hold the pack face down, while the right hand approaches the outer end to draw off the bottom card.

At this point, the left third finger gets busy. It moves inward and slides the bottom card along with it. Hence the right hand, in drawing off a card, is able to take the second card from the bottom—not the bottom card itself. The right hand deals the card face downward on the table and everyone supposes it to be the card that was shown on the bottom of the pack.

Moistening the left third finger will facilitate the operation of the "glide."

With this sleight, the magician can "change" a card or he can make a chosen card appear at any number from the bottom of the pack, simply by holding it back while others are drawn forth.

Second Method: This time, the right fingers do the work. The right hand approaches the outer end of the pack. The thumb rests on top; the fingers beneath. The right fingers push the bottom card back; then draw off the next card.

In both methods, the card can be drawn, when required, by the right fingers. If they want the pulled-back card, they simply stretch to get it and bring it out.

The "glide," while an easy sleight in either form, should not be neglected in practice. Its effectiveness depends upon doing it neatly. Fumbling will spoil any trick, and simply because the sleight is not hard to learn is no reason for performing it crudely.

17. THE FALSE COUNT A very simple and useful sleight. The performer wishes to count off some cards from the top of the pack and to actually take less than the audience supposes.

He does it thus. He draws off one card, saying "one." He places the card back on the pack and removes another with it, counting "two." The left thumb pushes each card to the right to assist the right hand in the removal.

In taking a third card, the magician simulates the previous movement, but he simply brushes the right hand cards upon the card that is on the pack, without removing it. The left thumb, at the same time, pulls back the card.

By this procedure, the magician can apparently count off twelve cards, really taking only nine. Three times during the course of the counting, the false motion is made.

With nine cards in his hand, the magician can count the packet to make it appear as twelve. He simply counts off three cards normally; makes the false count on number four; actually counts off the next card; then the false count; counts off another; then the false count; and finally counts off the remainder.

Make sure of the position of the cards, remembering that they are backs up. Practice the sleight, until you can do it naturally and easily. You will be surprised how simple it is— and how deceptive.

Chapter 4

CARD LOCATIONS

IN LOCATING CARDS, THERE ARE CERTAIN POINTS TO BE considered. A card, having been selected and replaced in the pack, is presumably lost. The chances of finding it again are —from the spectator's view—just about one in fifty-two.

It is true that very many tricks begin with the old formula: "Take a card." Perhaps the phrase has become hackneyed. Nevertheless, it is the usual beginning of many good tricks. If people want to see card tricks, they should expect to take cards.

After the card is taken, it is up to the performer to find it when needed. Card locations solve that problem. There are various types of locations. We can consider them in three groups.

First: The learning of a card. Through some method, the performer discovers the card by glancing through the pack after the card has been returned. This type of location is sometimes termed a "detection." It is not so effective as the controlling of a card, but it serves as well in certain tricks.

Second: The control of a card. The performer, by some system, keeps the card under his control, bringing it either to the top or the bottom of the pack. He does not necessarily know the name of the card. This type of location is usually followed by false shuffling.

Third: The forcing of a card. In this type of location the magician knows beforehand what card the spectator is going to take. The "force" serves purposes all its own. By use of it, the magician can predict the name of a card which is to be selected. The "force" also serves as a location, however, for it enables the magician to find a card any time after it is returned to the pack.

The special advantage of the "force" in locating cards is that with it, the spectators may be allowed to shuffle the pack themselves, thus strengthening the performer's own position when he shuffles for himself. This is also possible with a form of location known as the "glimpse," which is explained in this section.

Often, when the performer knows the name of a card, he can find it by the simple expedient of shuffling the pack dovetail fashion. He riffles the end of the pack that is toward himself and thus sights the card as it comes along. Cutting at that point, he can keep the card on the bottom or the top as he prefers.

This is a useful point to know in connection with card tricks where the performer is using some form of location other than the actual control of a chosen card.

1. THE DIVIDED PACK This is one of the simplest forms of card location ever devised. In fact, it is so simple that it has been relegated to beginners and its real merits have been forgotten.

Red and Black To explain the method in its primitive form requires only a few words. The pack is cut into two heaps. A card is selected at random from one heap. It is placed in the other heap. Looking through the second heap, the magician discovers the chosen card.

48

This is easy to do when one knows how the pack is divided. One heap contains red cards; the other heap contains black. Simple, isn't it? A red card shows up among the blacks or a black shows up among the reds—as the case may be.

Note that each heap may be shuffled prior to the drawing of a card. But should any spectator chance to look at the cards in his heap, he would easily find a clue to the trick.

Mixed Suits When we consider this idea in its more subtle forms, we discover real merit in it. The first stunt is to use the spades and hearts (mixed) in one heap; the clubs and diamonds (mixed) in the other. This means that a much closer inspection is necessary on the part of the spectator.

Odd and Even A further improvement is to pay no attention to suit whatever. Use all *odd* cards (ace, three, five, seven, nine, jack, king) in one heap; use all *even* cards (two, four, six, eight, ten, queen) in the other. That makes detection highly unlikely.

Mixed Odds and Evens In its most elaborate form, the trick utilizes the *even* spades and hearts and the *odd* clubs and diamonds in one heap; the other heap consists of the *odd* spades and hearts and the *even* clubs and diamonds. This makes the system virtually undetectable.

For practical purposes, however, the use of odds in one section and evens in the other will be all that the performer may require.

Now it is obvious that the trick will work both ways: given two heaps of different kinds of cards, one or more cards may be transferred from heap A to heap B; or from heap B to heap A. Examination of both heaps will show any "strangers" in their midst. Thus the performer is not limited to the choice of a single card.

Complete Pack Method Let us consider the two-heap

idea with the pack all together. The top portion of the pack consists of, say, odds. The lower portion consists of evens. Spreading the pack, the magician requests the selection of a card. If one is taken from the top half of the pack, he keeps on spreading and allows the card to be put back in the bottom part. If one is taken from the bottom portion, the pack is closed and spread again near the top, so the card goes in there.

This is done with two or more cards; then the pack is cut a few times. Upon looking at the faces of the cards—even while the spectators are watching—the magician can immediately find the chosen cards.

Complete Pack with Shuffles   To make the trick more deceptive, we shall explain a way of using this principle in which the pack is genuinely cut in four heaps before the selection of cards; and actually shuffled in dovetail fashion after the chosen cards are replaced!

Arrange group A (consisting of even reds and odd blacks) on top of group B (consisting of odd reds and even blacks). Remember the bottom card of group A—say the ten of diamonds. Or the joker may be placed at that point.

Spread the pack slightly and cut at the key card. That makes two heaps, A and B. Cut each of those heaps, making two A heaps and two B heaps. In assembling, gather the heaps A, B, A, B from bottom to top. The A heap with the ten of diamonds should be the upper A heap. Also note the bottom card of the upper B heap.

Now cards are selected and replaced. This time, you are dealing with four groups. They must be considered as the cards are replaced. Simply see to it that the card goes in a group of the other variety.

When the chosen cards are back in the pack, spread a trifle to find the ten of diamonds and cut there. Now, in dovetailing,

50

let the right hand cards drop more rapidly than the left. As soon as the bottom card of the upper B heap (say the four of spades) appears, retain it and let the left hand cards fall until they are well exhausted. Then finish the shuffle. This simply segregates the A and B heaps. You are ready to look for the chosen cards.

2. THE NEW PACK   This is one of those opportune tricks that no card conjuror should neglect when the occasion permits it. It is particularly useful when performing at a card table. A new pack is often presented to the magician and then he has his chance.

A pack of cards is taken from the case. It is spread along the table. Persons are asked to draw cards. The magician's head is turned away. As soon as cards have been removed, he closes the pack without looking at it—sweeping the cards together.

Again he spreads the pack and asks for the replacement of the chosen cards. This being done, he sweeps the pack up without even glancing at it.

Nothing could seem fairer than this. The magician does not even know how many cards were chosen. But by spreading the pack before him and concentrating, he manages to remove several cards, which he lays faces down. The chosen cards are named. Those cards are turned up. They are the chosen ones!

New packs are always arranged in sequence of suits. Nowadays the suits are usually in order from ace to king. Thus when cards are taken—the pack closed—the pack reopened—the selected cards naturally go back at new positions and it is a simple matter to learn their identity by simply looking through the pack! For they are out of place.

The pack may be cut once or twice during the trick; that does not disturb the rotation. Afterward, the pack should be shuffled immediately to dispose of the clue that would give away the method.

3. EASY LOCATIONS   (*With Puzzling Additions*)

Bottom Card Location   This is one of the oldest types of card location. We are describing it, however, because it has many useful variations and can be made to deceive the shrewdest spectator if handled in the proper manner.

Basically, the trick is simply a division of the pack into two heaps. A card is taken from the top of the lower heap, noted, and transferred to the upper heap. The cut is then completed. After a few cuts of the pack, the magician looks through the cards and discovers the selected one.

This is accomplished by first sighting the bottom card of the pack. When the selected card is transferred from the lower heap to the upper and the cut completed, the known (bottom) card naturally comes on top of the selected card. Cutting does not separate those two cards. It is easy for the magician to discover the chosen card.

Top Card Location   Now let us note some variations to this idea which the average man of a few card tricks does not know. First is the subterfuge of noting the *top* card of the pack instead of the bottom. To facilitate this, the magician may actually note the bottom card and shuffle it to the top before placing the pack on the table. The pack is cut; it is divided into two heaps. A card is noted while being transferred from the lower heap to the upper. The magician tells the spectator to complete the cut—and requests him to mix the cards of the lower heap before he does so!

The shuffle puts the bottom card out of commission and kills the spectator's pet theory (if he has it) that the bottom card is of help to the magician.

52

Top and Bottom Location   Another factor which is not realized—even by magicians—is that the pack can be shuffled when the bottom card or the top card serve as locators. Yes, it can be shuffled—if you pick your shuffler.

The average person does not shuffle a pack thoroughly. Noting such a person, the magician can give him the pack for shuffling and the chances of the two cards (locator and chosen) being separated is very slight. This applies to those who shuffle by the overhand method. The dovetail shuffle, if thorough, is more apt to spoil the trick.

But this leads us to the combined location in which the magician knows *both* the top card and the bottom one. When the pack is cut into two heaps and the chosen card transferred from lower to upper, the completion of the cut puts it *between* two known cards.

The magician can either find it as the card above the original top card or the card below the original bottom card. In other words, the wizard has caused the formation of a little cluster of three cards—the center one being the selected card.

Ordinary shuffling is not apt to disturb this group. Upon looking through the pack, the magician will usually find the desired card right between the other two. But supposing the shuffle is quite a thorough one. The chosen card may drift away from one of its locators, but it has very little chance of leaving both of them.

For instance: let us consider a group formed by the six of spades, ace of hearts and six of diamonds (from top to bottom). The six of spades is the original bottom card; the ace of hearts is the chosen card; the six of diamonds is the original top card. If the cards appear in that position after the shuffle, it is obvious that the ace of hearts is the card the magician wants.

Now suppose he finds the two locating sixes well apart. Beneath the six of spades is the king of clubs; above the six of diamonds is the ace of hearts. He knows that the chosen card is either the king of clubs or the ace of hearts. The magician then uses both those cards in whatever trick he is performing. For instance, he can slide one card to the top of the pack and the other to the bottom. Then he strikes the pack and turns up the top card. If it is recognized as the chosen card, well and good. If not, the magician "remembers" that the blow knocks the card to the bottom—not to the top, so he shows the bottom card to be the chosen one.

4. THE MASTER CARD LOCATION This trick was highly advertised when it appeared a few years ago and it is still known to only a very few. It is a most convincing method of discovering a chosen card. The pack is shuffled by a spectator. The magician spreads the pack face down. A spectator touches a card. Before he has a chance to remove it, the magician puts the pack right in the spectator's hands and lets him turn up the card while the pack is in his own possession. He does not even remove the card from the pack. Then he cuts the pack as often as he wishes; yet the magician, looking through the pack, learns the name of the selected card.

The operation is quite ingenious. Upon receiving the shuffled pack, the magician notes the bottom card by turning the pack slightly toward himself. He begins to spread the cards from hand to hand. He counts them as he does so. Thus, when the spectator touches a card, the magician knows just how far down it is from the top.

He gives out the pack with impunity. For so long as the spectator cuts the cards with single cuts only, the selected card will always be the same number below the card that was on the bottom of the pack—the number counted from the bottom!

All the magician has to do when he gets the pack is spread the cards with the faces toward himself. He looks for the card he knows (the original bottom card) and counts down to the selected card. If he comes to the bottom of the pack during his count, he continues the count from the top.

Cutting the pack—in single cuts—does not change the rotation and the relationship of the known card to the chosen one will remain a constant number.

In utilizing this card location, the performer should practice counting cards as he spreads them. There is much to be gained by doing the counting in a rapid, smooth manner. With a little practice, it is quite an easy matter to count the spreading cards by threes instead of singly. The magician begins his counting as he tells the spectator to touch any card. As a result, the selected card will be well down in the pack.

If desired, a spectator may be allowed to simply peek at the corner of a card and the magician may slide the cards along further, allowing a choice of a second card. In this case he starts a second count or continues the first one. This is one of the best of all methods fer determining the name of a selected card.

5. THE SLIDE OUT   While this form of card location is an old one, it is virtually unknown to the present day magician. We are describing it here, with improvements, because it is a good, reliable method of controlling a selected card. It serves the same purpose as Blackstone's "Card Control."*

A certain amount of skill is necessary in the maneuver, as it brings a selected card to the bottom of the pack. Nevertheless,

*Explained in Blackstone's "Modern Card Tricks and Secrets of Magic."

the movements are so natural and so simple that the method is by no means difficult to learn.

Simply spread the pack between the hands and ask that a card be selected. This card is returned to the center of the pack. Then the left thumb draws a few cards to the left so that they

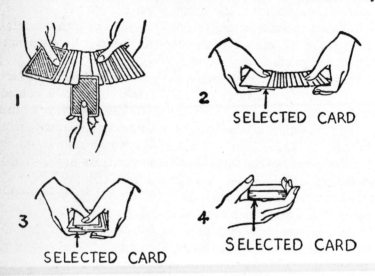

THE SLIDE OUT

(1) Selected card returned to the pack. (2) The selected card drawn beneath the spread. (3) The selected card at the bottom. (4) Final stage of the sleight.

cover the selected one, as though making sure that it is lost in the middle of the pack.

The spread, at this juncture, is quite wide. The pack has been opened slightly to admit the return of the chosen card. The right fingers, reaching beneath, slide the chosen card to the right. This is hidden by the cards which the left thumb has

56

drawn over the chosen one. A short pull by the right fingers and the chosen card is clear of the pack—beneath it.

Now the pack is closed by bringing the hands together. It is no trick at all to let the selected card glide along the bottom as a free agent until it safely arrives on the bottom of the pack.

The maneuver may be repeated with another selected card —in fact as many cards may be used as required for the particular trick. Each one glides to the bottom. There they may be easily controlled.

Some readers may prefer this system to the Blackstone "Card Control," although the "Card Control" is unquestionably the superior method. It is interesting to compare the two, however, and good results may be obtained by alternating them.

In the "Slide Out," the magician may start to close the spread by pulling a few cards to the left; then he can begin to spread the cards again, telling the chooser to note that his card is actually in the center of the pack.

What the spectator sees is one of the cards which the left thumb drew over. Seeing only the back of the card, he takes it for granted that it is really his card. By diverting attention in this manner, the magician has an excuse for spreading the pack, which facilitates the sliding of the chosen card to the right. Then the pack is closed with a quick movement and the selected card goes to the bottom.

6. THE PUSH THROUGH A card is selected from the pack. The magician holds the pack in his left hand and squares it so that all the cards are well together. He riffles the outer end of the pack so that the selected card may be inserted. This card projects—so the magician pushes it squarely into the pack.

This being done, he divides the pack into two heaps and proceeds with a dovetail shuffle. Everything is natural—in fact, the magician goes to great pains to show that there is no possible way for him to control the chosen card. Yet that is exactly what he does.

It's all in the "push." When the chosen card is inserted, the end projects, as has been mentioned. The magician pushes the card into the pack; in doing this, he strikes it rather forcibly,

THE PUSH THROUGH

Left: Selected card returned and left projecting. Center: The right hand strikes the card into the pack. Right: The chosen card projecting at the back.

As a result, the card now projects from the inner end of the pack, where it cannot be seen by the spectators.

When the pack is divided into two heaps for the shuffle, the magician simply uses the projecting end of the selected card as a tab by which he can lift the upper portion. In shuffling, he lets this card fall first, thus placing it on the bottom of the pack.

If the cards are held slightly loose, the card will push through more readily. Remember that the strong part of this trick lies in its apparent fairness. It may be done deliberately, with good effect.

7. THE PUSH BACK A very neat form of location. Riffle the pack and allow a card to be selected. Raise the upper portion of the pack with the right hand so the card may be replaced upon the lower heap. Now comes the important move.

In setting the upper portion on the lower, bring the inner end down first. Let the tip of the right thumb rest upon the chosen card.

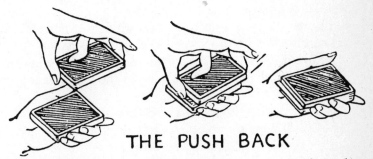

THE PUSH BACK

How the right thumb pushes back the top card of the lower heap (the selected card) while placing the upper half of the pack in position.

As the top portion of the pack is a trifle advanced, the hand is naturally drawn back so that the front edge of the pack will be even. Due to the pressure of the thumb, the chosen card moves backward as this action is performed.

The entire movement is covered by the upper heap. The front of the pack is tilted a trifle upward. The chosen card projects half an inch at the rear of the pack, but it is not observed.

The right hand squares the pack very carefully. With the pack squared and the chosen card presumably safely buried, the performer is ready to execute the dovetail shuffle. He can bring the selected card either to the top or bottom. For the bottom, he lifts its projecting end when he cuts the pack. For the top, he lifts all cards above the projection.

8. A NEAT LOCATION

A card having been selected, the magician squares the pack and holds it for the reception of the chosen card. He lifts up a large portion of the pack and invites the chooser to return his card. When this is done, the magician drops the rest of the pack on top.

In this natural procedure, he keeps the location of the chosen card. When he drops the upper portion, he lets it fall slightly toward himself, so the upper section projects inward. He immediately tilts the hand forward so the cards slide flush at the front.

But the card directly above the chosen one will not slide forward. It will remain, projecting inward. When the magician shuffles by the dovetail system, he uses this tab to lift off the upper half of the pack.

In shuffling, he lets the top card of the lower half be among the last to fall. It being the selected card, the result is that the performer brings the chosen card to the top of the pack where it is in just the position where he can use it.

9. THE FAN LOCATION

In this location, the pack is fanned or spread in the customary manner for a person to select a card. When it is replaced, the magician uses a very clever subterfuge. He holds the pack fanned rather closely, in the right hand. Thus it is impossible for the spectator to push the card entirely into the pack.

The magician may use his left hand to help—if the spectator pushes the card only about half way in, the performer can re-

Warrenville Public Library District

09/15/14 07:41PM

Renew Online, by Phone or Self-Check

http://ipac.warrenville.com

1.630.393.1171

PATRON: **********2386

Tim Gunn's fashion bible : the fascinati
34901635999914   Due date: 10/13/

Haute dogs : recipes for delicious hot d
34901636190778   Due date: 10/13/

TOTAL: 2

Thank You!

mark that it should go farther in, suiting the words with the action.

When the card is nearly in the pack, the magician turns slightly to the left and closes the fan by striking the left edge of the pack against the palm of his left hand. Even though he has pushed the chosen card well in, it will still project slightly. It forms a tab which can be easily located.

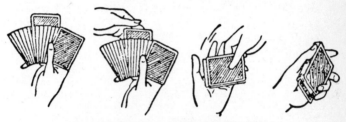

THE FAN LOCATION

Selected card inserted in the fan is pushed in almost flush. The squaring of the pack leaves it projecting.

Note that at this point, the end of the pack from which the card projects is turned away from the spectators. The magician simply takes the pack and shuffles it in dovetail fashion. He catches the projecting card with his right thumb, separating the pack at that point. Letting the chosen card fall first, puts it on the bottom of the pack, from which position it is easily controlled.

10. A CARD DETECTION This is a simple method of learning the name of a chosen card. It is particularly useful as it leaves the card in a very advantageous position—on the bottom of the pack, where the magician may learn the name of the card and reveal it as he sees fit.

Give the pack to a spectator. Tell him to shuffle it. Tell him to deal off any number of cards, faces up, one by one, making a heap—and to note the last card dealt. You turn your back while he does this. Suppose he deals eight and the last card is the five of spades. You do not know this and you tell him to replace the cards on the pack, remembering both the card and the number.

You turn away with the pack and work with it a few moments. Then you return it to the spectator, saying that you have mixed the cards but have not discovered the chosen one. Ask him to deal the same number that he dealt before—faces up—but not to remember any new card—to keep the name of the old card constantly in mind.

He does this while your back is turned and you ask him to replace the dealt cards upon the bottom of the pack. He is apt to notice that his card does not appear this time; that is natural, because you mixed the cards.

Again you take the cards and mix them, either by looking at them or by holding them behind your back. Then you discover his card—either by showing it to him on the bottom of the pack or by producing it in some clever manner.

How do you get the card? Simply enough. Suppose the spectator dealt twelve cards and put them on the top; then dealt twelve and put them on the bottom. The twelfth—chosen—card would naturally wind up on the bottom of the pack. That's the way you do the trick—but you do not work it so baldly.

When you first receive the pack, count off a number of cards from the bottom and put them on the top. That is done after the spectator's first deal. Remember the number of cards you use—say sixteen. After the second deal by the spectator, count off the same number of cards—sixteen in this case—but this time take them from the top of the pack and put them on the bottom.

This has the same effect as the simple procedure described above. Perhaps, in reading it, you may think it won't work. But it does work—every time—and that is the beauty of it. Just follow the directions as specified and you will get the chosen card on the bottom of the pack where you want it.

11. THE PICK-UP HEAPS This is a bold form of card location, but a deceptive one, if properly practiced. The magician divides the pack into three heaps—or allows someone else to do so. A card is selected and placed on one of the heaps. The magician drops that heap on another heap and drops the third heap on top. He appears to bury the selected card in the pack.

Actually, he is bringing the card to the top. It is done this way. Pick up the heap with the chosen card and drop that heap on another heap. As you do so, retain a few of the top cards between the tips of your thumb and fingers. In reaching for the odd heap, simply carry those extra cards along (the chosen card being on top of them) and let them fall on the final heap as you carry it to the pack.

This requires smartness of action, even though no special skill is necessary. There is an important point that adds much. If you intend to use your right hand, make sure that the spectators are mostly to your right. Your hand, tilting slightly in their direction, covers the carried cards very effectively.

If the spectators are on your left, use the left hand to execute the three-heap pick-up.

12. SURPASSO This is the title of a remarkable card detection that is one of the newest and best ideas in card conjuring. It approaches the impossible when well performed; and the trick is not difficult, although it requires close attention to detail.

Anyone removes a pack of cards from its case and gives the pack a shuffle. Then the person selects a card and puts it face down in the case. Following the magician's instructions, the person then inserts the pack, seeing to it that the

SURPASSO

Left: Selected card is first placed in case. Center: Then the pack itself is inserted. Right: Selected card discovered projecting.

selected card is buried amongst the others. This is accomplished by making a little space in the pack to receive the chosen card.

The magician takes the case as the spectator closes it and retires to the opposite side of the room. He looks at the case; then at the spectator. He removes the cards from the case, runs through the pack and produces the selected card!

The secret is a simple one. Using the usual style flap case, the pack, when pushed in, has a tendency to shove the single card further down. To make sure of this, the magician should approach and take the pack just as soon as the spectator has the pack well in. If the pack fits the case rather tightly, so much the better.

Across the room, the magician inverts the case and taps the flap end against his hand. This evens the pack a bit. When he removes the pack from the case, the magician grips it firmly and he will discover one card projecting a fraction of an inch from the lower end. That card is the selected card. He takes it from the pack. The use of the case makes the trick good, because no one can see the projecting card.

13. AN EASY FORCE This idea has many uses. It is explained here in a simple and effective form. The magician lays a pack on the table. He writes something on a sheet of paper. He ask someone to cut the pack at any point. The paper is laid between the two portions.

When the upper half of the pack is lifted, the spectators are asked to note the card on its face—suppose it is the queen of clubs. The paper is unfolded. It bears the name "queen of clubs."

This is accomplished by simply noting the bottom card of the pack after a shuffle. That is the name which the magician writes on the sheet of paper. It does not matter where the pack is cut. The magician simply picks up the lower half of the pack and completes the cut by dropping it on the top half— but he inserts the sheet of paper as he does so.

Thus it is the bottom card—the known card—which comes on top of the sheet of paper. But the method is so natural and so subtle that persons will be positive the magician put the paper at an unknown spot near the center of the pack.

For ordinary forcing or location purposes, the magician may note secretly the top card of the pack; then ask someone to cut the cards and to complete the cut by leaving the upper portion at an angle. Then a spectator is allowed to look at the card immediately below the break. This is the card that the wizard knows; but people will not realize it. That card can be discovered later—after a shuffle.

AN EASY FORCE

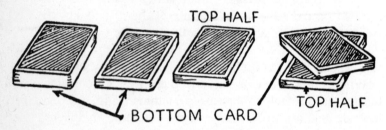

Known card on bottom of pack. Top half removed; lower half placed on it. Bottom card arrives at the center, ready for selection.

14. THE JOKER FORCE This is by no means a new idea; but it is a very useful one. It enables the magician to learn the name of a card before the card is drawn.

It begins after a borrowed pack has been shuffled. The magician takes the pack, turns the bottom card toward himself and remarks that he must remove the joker. He spreads the cards from the bottom; when he reaches the joker, he discards it and lays the pack face down upon the table.

The pack is now cut into three heaps. Choice is given of one. The top card of the heap is noted by a spectator. Strange though it may seem, the magician knows that card and no matter how often the pack may be shuffled he can always look through and find it.

The trick begins with the removal of the joker. As he runs through the bottom cards of the pack, in his search for the joker, the magician slyly slides the top card a trifle to the left—just far enough so he can see its index corner. After removing the joker, he squares the pack and divides it into three heaps. He lifts off two-thirds of the face-down pack and places the large upper portion to the right of the lower. He then lifts half of the upper portion and puts it between the two heaps.

This tricky cut is seldom noticed. It puts the top of the pack in the middle of the heaps, although one would normally suppose the top portion was at the right.

When the magician asks that a heap be chosen, the spectator usually obliges by taking the center one. He is told to look at the top card of the heap—the very card that the magician knows.

Suppose that the center heap is not chosen? Very well. The magician tells the person who takes an end heap to remove it. Then he remarks that there are two heaps left. One must be eliminated. Which does the person want?

If the desired heap is touched, the magician says: "You want that one? Well, that eliminates this one." If the wrong heap is indicated, the magician's response is: "So that's the one you want eliminated. Well, that leaves this one."

An interesting trick performed by the joker force is to ascribe wonderful powers to the joker itself—a good excuse for removing it from the pack. When the center heap is chosen (whether the spectator wants it or not!) the magician tells the chooser to push the top card off the heap and on to the table.

Then the card is touched with the joker. The magician pretends to hold conversation with the joker. It tells him the name of the card and the magician announces that name. To prove the joker was correct, he uses the joker to flip the single card face up on the table and the statement is seen to be true.

15. THE FORCE LOCATION This form of card location involves a simple type of card force. It is designed to work to the performer's advantage whether or not the right card is actually selected by the spectator.

Briefly, the magician spreads the pack and asks that a card be selected. This card is removed and replaced in the pack, which is fairly closed. The magician later discovers or names the selected card.

The first thing the magician does is to note the bottom card of the pack. He draws off the lower portion and transfers it to the top, keeping the two sections slightly apart so that he can handle the known card.

In spreading the pack, he pushes this card a trifle forward so that it projects more than the others and is the logical card which the average person would select. If that card is taken, well and good. Everything is as the magician wishes it.

Now suppose the known card is not selected. In most instances the chooser will pick a card quite close to it. The magician can visually count to the card that the spectator draws. It may, for example, be three cards below the known one—or five cards above. It may often be the card next to the known one.

Under such circumstances, the magician says to the spectator: "Don't remove the card from the pack—just look at its corner." This enables the magician to close the pack, holding the chosen card at its relative position from the known one. Needless to say, the chosen card may be easily discovered by looking for the known card and counting to it. The pack is not shuffled—unless a false method is used.

Should the spectator pick a card well away from the card which the magician desired to force, another procedure is available. The performer lets the spectator take the card clear of the deck. When it is about to be replaced, the wizard raises the pack at the known card, forming a space for the return of the selected one.

This brings the chosen card next to the known card and the matter of locating the chosen card is simplified. In a great percentage of cases, the known card will be the one selected and in such instances, this additional action is not necessary.

Nevertheless, it gives the magician an excellent way of avoiding the embarrassment that follows the selection of the wrong card when a force is attempted. The old style procedure was to do another trick when the force missed; but it is much more satisfactory to utilize the forcing card as a locator when the emergency calls for it.

16. BEHIND THE BACK This is an excellent method for forcing a card. The magician holds a shuffled pack behind his back. He lets a person lift off some cards. The magician asks that the next card be noted. This is done. The card is then replaced; the pack is shuffled by the audience. Nevertheless, the magician knows the name of the card.

He manages this by removing the card from the pack *before* he begins the trick. If the magician simply wants to know the name of any card that the audience may take, he removes any card and notes its identity. If he wants a certain card taken, he removes that card from the pack. The magician tucks this card beneath his belt, behind his back, the face of the card being outward.

Tricks are performed while that card is missing from the pack, no one realizing that it is absent. When the performer wishes to have the card selected, he turns his back and tells someone to put the pack face down in his left hand; then to lift a number of cards.

As soon as the cards are raised, the magician swings toward the spectator, with some pertinent remark, such as: "You took off some cards, didn't you?" This hides the left hand momentarily. Raising the hand to his belt, the magician draws away the hidden card so that it lies on top of the cards that are in his left hand.

Turning away again, the magician extends his left hand behind his back and asks the spectator to look at the next card—that is, the card now on top of the left hand packet. Inasmuch as it is totally impossible for the magician to have seen the card, there is no suspicion. This card is noted; then the pack is shuffled.

In brief, the magician has simply added his held-out card in such a way that it is logically selected and he can proceed with the trick without danger of detection.

This method can be used in a different way, however. When the spectator lifts a bunch of cards, the magician can turn and tell him to glance at the bottom card of the group he has taken. While the spectator is doing so, the magician adds the extra card. Turning his back, he asks that the spectator's group be replaced. This is done. The chosen card is now directly above the card that the performer knows. Hence the discovery of the selected card is not a difficult matter.

In this method, the pack should be cut a few times behind

the magician's back—not shuffled. This is merely a variation of the forcing idea and is mentioned because it has occasional use.

17. THE GLIMPSE

This maneuver is aptly named, because in practice, the magician glimpses the index corner of a card after it has been returned to the pack. Thus learning the name of the card, he can allow the pack to be shuffled, yet can find it when he wants it.

First Method: Simply insert the left little finger beneath the card after it has been returned to the pack. The finger is at the right, inner corner. Raise the upper portion of the pack slightly and shift it a trifle to the left. At the same time bring the left edge of the pack straight up. Note the index corner with a downward glance and immediately close the pack, removing the little finger from between the two portions.

Second Method: Riffle the front edge of the pack and ask a person to insert his finger. When he does so, tell him to note the card above his finger. Let the rest of the pack fall with a quick riffle, but press the ball of your left forefinger against the outer right corner so a space remains there.

The left thumb, on top of the pack, pushes the upper portion a trifle to the right as the left hand turns the pack face up, toward yourself. This gives you a glimpse of the selected card and the right hand immediately takes the pack, bottom up, closing the space. The right hand offers the pack to a spectator for shuffling.

Third Method: This is for sighting the top card of the pack, after the cards have been shuffled. It is useful in certain tricks. Hold the pack in the left hand. The fingers are beneath; the thumb is across the top.

During a gesture of the left hand, the thumb pushes the top card a fraction of an inch to the right and a trifle forward. The left hand turns the end of the pack almost straight up and the index corner of the top card is sighted.

A good finish to this movement is to square the pack by tapping it upon the table—a logical excuse for the movement of the pack.

Another way of utilizing this glimpse is to perform it while transferring the pack from the left hand to the right. The left

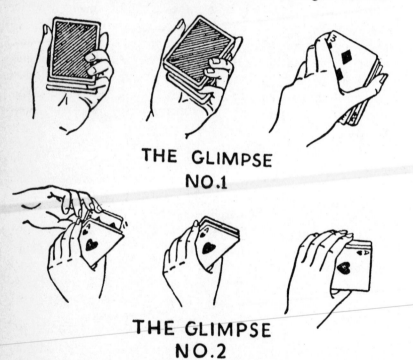

THE GLIMPSE
NO.1

THE GLIMPSE
NO.2

The methods of glimpsing a card in the center of the pack are depicted here.

hand turns the pack almost face upward, the thumb pushing the top card out. The fingers of the right hand cover the tell-tale corner and the right hand grips the pack, fingers below, thumb above, turning the pack face down.

Chapter 5

CARD DISCOVERIES

AFTER A CARD HAS BEEN SELECTED AND REPLACED IN in the pack, the performer naturally discovers it in order to complete the trick which he is exhibiting.

The simplest form of card discovery is to pick the card out of the pack. That is effective when the spectators are sure that the magician has no way of finding the card. To discover one card out of a possible fifty-two is a good trick in itself.

But to get effective results in card magic, the performer should utilize various surprising methods of producing a chosen card after it has been lost in the pack. Such methods are known as card discoveries.

This section includes a list of effective discoveries following the selection of a card. The reader may choose those which interest him the most and by using them in connection with locations, he will be able to form a most surprising repertoire.

The usual steps before a card discovery are: the selection of a card; its replacement; its control or location by a method known to the magician; the shuffling of the pack (by false shuffles or cuts). Then the stage is set for the surprising appearance of the selected card.

1. THE KNOCK OUT An effective conclusion to a card trick. This method is well-known, but is mentioned here because it is always good and also because of its variations. Note the points of difference in the methods.

The magician holds the pack in his left hand. He strikes it with his right or allows a spectator to perform that action. The result: the only card that remains in the magician's hand is the one that was selected beforehand by a spectator.

First Method: The selected card is brought to the bottom of the pack. Hold the pack firmly in the left hand, fingers beneath and thumb on top. Hold it at one corner. The pack is face down. When the cards are struck, all are knocked from the hand except the bottom (selected) card.

Second Method: This time the selected card is brought to the top of the pack, which is held face up. The blow works the same, but the selected card is face up, staring at the spectators. This is a better effect.

Third Method: The card is brought to the top. The pack is held face downward. The spectator is asked to strike the pack *upward*. As a result, cards are scattered everywhere. The magician's hand goes upward with the blow so that only the selected card remains, facing the spectators.

2. CARD FROM THE POCKET This is an old method of discovering a selected card; but it is given here with a puzzling addition. The pack is placed in the performer's inside pocket. Someone is told to reach in and draw out a card. He does so—and he brings out the selected card!

The answer is that the selected card is on top of the pack. By hurrying the person, the magician causes him to draw off the top card—the only one which he can easily and naturally grasp. The top of the pack is outward in the pocket.

Now for the improvement. Two selected cards. The magician shuffles the pack and puts it in his pocket. Reaching in, he draws out one of the selected cards.

Then, as an added feature, he takes the pack from his pocket and lets anyone shuffle it. Back it goes in the pocket. A spectator is told to seize a card from the pack. He does so— out comes the second selected card!

How does the magician get around the shuffle? Simply enough. He has both selected cards on top. He draws out one himself. When he brings out the pack to be shuffled, he leaves the other selected card in his pocket. It goes on top of the pack again, when the magician replaces the pack. That's why the grabbing spectator gets it.

3. ANY NUMBER Here we make a chosen card appear at any number in the pack after the pack has been shuffled. Suppose nine is the number given. The chosen card is on top of the pack, brought there by the magician. He counts off nine cards one by one—this count reversed their order. He shows the ninth card. It is not the chosen one. So the performer puts the nine cards back on the pack.

He recalls that he forgot the magic riffle. So he riffles the pack and again counts to nine. Due to the reversed order, the chosen card shows up at the required number—in this instance, just nine cards from the top of the pack.

Now for an improvement on the old idea. Suppose nine is given, with the chosen card on top. Count off eight (reversing their order). Drop the ninth on the table and ask the person to look at it. While attention is directed there, the eight cards are brought back to the pack by the right hand. The right fingers push the chosen card forward. The left hand, tilting to the right, allows the card to come face-up on the rest of

76

the pack; rather, the left hand puts the pack face down on the chosen card. Swinging to its normal position, the left hand receives the other cards on top of the pack, as they should be.

The performer does this automatically. It is all finished by the time the spectator has discovered that the ninth card is not the one he selected. So the magician puts that card on top of the pack and resorts to his magic riffle.

Then comes the surprise. Counting slowly to nine, the magician reveals the chosen card at the desired number and furthermore the chosen card is face up—just a little token of the potency of the wizard's riffle!

One important fact should be noted—for this trick and all others that involve reversed cards. Only perform such effects with packs that have a white margin on the backs. Otherwise, there will be difficulty. Most good packs have the required white margins.

Any slight unevenness of the pack will not betray a reversed card, if white margins are used. But with packs that have a design running solid to the border, reversed card tricks should be avoided.

4. A REVERSED CARD A card having been selected and returned to the pack, the magician starts a search for it. He finds a card and lays it face upward on top of the pack.

"That's your card, isn't it?" he asks.

"No," is the reply.

"What!" exclaims the mystifier. "Not the six of spades? I'll have to try again."

He removes the seven of diamonds and thrusts it back into the pack, which he shuffles. Then he turns the pack face downward and spreads it. One card appears face up. It proves to be the card selected.

The Method: The magician easily finds the chosen card by whatever system he chooses to use. But he draws it from the pack in back of the six of spades—that is, he holds the two cards as one and instantly lays them face upward on top of the pack.

Finding that the six of spades is not correct, the magician tilts the pack upward so that only the faces of cards can be seen. He takes the six of spades from the top of the pack and puts it properly among the other cards.

But this time, he manages the six of spades alone—leaving the chosen card face up on top of the pack. A short easy shuffle—keeping the faces of the cards toward the spectators —puts the chosen card in the midst of the pack—face up, ready for the finish.

5. ONE REVERSED CARD   An easy reversed card trick, depending upon one simple move which can be made slowly without fear of detection. A chosen card is brought to the

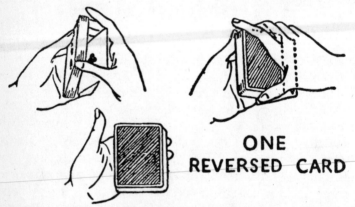

ONE
REVERSED CARD

Movements of shifting the top card of the pack so it lies face up on the bottom.

top of the pack. The magician shuffles with the faces of the cards toward the spectators and he keeps the chosen card on top of the pack.

Completing the shuffle, he grips the top card with the fingers of his left hand. At the same time, the right hand (thumb at one end, fingers at the other) lifts the pack a trifle upward and forward and turns it face down.

The left hand goes flat as the pack is turned, so the magician simply lays the pack on that single, face-up card. All that is now necessary is to cut the pack; then spread it on the table. The chosen card will be seen face up in the midst of the face-down cards.

6. THREE REVERSED CARDS   This is a very bewildering card trick. The magician apparently causes three selected cards to reverse themselves so they lie faces up at different parts of the pack.

The first card selected is brought to the top of the pack. The magician places it face up on the bottom (as described in the preceding "One Reversed Card" trick). He leaves the card on the bottom.

Now he spreads the pack (watching the bottom card) and has two more cards taken, by persons well apart. Squaring the pack he walks from person three to person two. As he does so, he turns the pack over in his left hand, so the single card is face up on bottom. He tells person two to insert his card at any spot, calling attention to the fact that the pack is squared so the card's position cannot be noted. The card goes in face down. Thus, like the card on the bottom, it is inverted or reversed.

Going back to person three, the magician, with a swing of his hand, brings the real top of the pack uppermost again.

He lifts a few cards off with his right hand and transfers them to the bottom, saying: "When I cut like this, put your card on."

Lifting a few more, the magician allows the placement of the third chosen card. He drops the right hand cards upon it and immediately brings the card to the top of the pack.*

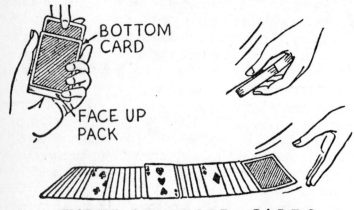

THREE REVERSED CARDS

Upper Left: How the pack is held face up, with one selected card inverted upon it. Second card is being inserted.

Upper Right: Third selected card projecting on the top of pack.

Bottom: The result—three cards face up.

The result now is that one chosen card is on top of the pack. The others are reversed but buried. The magician holds the pack across his right hand, with the thumb on top. He pushes the top card slightly forward and lets the pack slide along the table—or better, along the floor.

This maneuver, if properly done, causes the top card to turn over on the pack, due to the air pressure. It travels along with the pack and seems to bob out from some unexpected

*The "Revolving Pass" is useful at this point.

spot. At the same time, the spreading pack reveals the other two chosen cards, each lying face up amidst the pack.

It looks like a triple reverse and the fact that the cards are far apart has a marked effect upon those who witness it. This trick should be carefully rehearsed, as it contains many points that must be remembered, even though it has been simplified in method so that any performer of ordinary ability can demonstrate it without recourse to unusual dexterity.

7. OUT OF THE HAT This is a great finish for a card trick. Cards are selected and replaced in the pack, which is shuffled. The magician handles the deck a while; then spies a felt hat, into which he drops the pack. He holds the hat with the brim upward. He flips the crown of the hat with his forefinger. Out come the selected cards, sailing toward the ceiling!

There is no great difficulty in this trick. It may be performed with one or more selected cards. They are brought to the top of the pack or to the bottom. In either instance, the magician is set for the hat trick. When he drops the pack into the hat, he keeps the opening of the hat toward himself. He lets the pack go into one section of the hat; but he retains the selected cards and slides them into the other section of the hat.

Holding the hat above the spectators' line of vision, the magician makes a sharp flip against the crown of the hat. But he chooses the side where the selected cards are located. The force of the flip causes the cards to fly out of the hat in a most mysterious fashion. The hat is immediately tilted forward and the rest of the pack is allowed to slide out on the table.

8. BLACKSTONE'S CUT TRICK This is one of the finest of all card discoveries. Two cards are selected by the audience. The magician shuffles the pack after the cards are returned. He riffles the end of the pack and asks a third person to insert another card, face upward, at any point in the pack.

This is done. The third person retains his hold on the face-up card. The magician withdraws the entire pack, with the exception of two cards—the one above the inserted card and the one below.

Holding these three cards, the conjuror calls for the names of the selected cards. The names given, he turns over the

BLACKSTONE'S CUT TRICK

(1) Pack with one chosen card on top, other on bottom.
(2) Pack cut. Little finger retains the break.
(3) Riffling for the face-up insertion of an odd card.
(4) Drawing off from the break, showing face-up card.
(5) Top half replaced upon the lower.
(6) Pack spread to find inserted card between chosen ones.

three cards in his hand. This reveals the two selected cards! The spectator has thrust his face-up card between them!

The Secret: The two selected cards are first received in the pack and one is brought to the top; the other to the bottom. This is done by a card location system and is aided by false shuffles.

Now the magician cuts the pack by drawing off some of the lower bottom cards, to the rear, with his right hand. He puts the lower half on the upper half. This brings the selected cards together, but the left little finger holds a space between them. The cut should be made so that the two cards are fairly near the bottom of the pack as it now stands.

Riffling the pack at the outer end (with the right fingers) the magician invites the insertion of the odd face-up card. If it happens to go in the space between the two selected cards, well and good. But the magician is riffling rapidly to reach that space and the card often goes in above it.

With his right hand, the magician simply grips the upper portion of the pack (all cards above the break held by the left little finger). His right thumb is below; fingers above. He draws back the entire portion of the pack until it is free of the face-up card which the spectator is holding. Then he slaps that portion down upon the face-up card.

This movement is natural, sure and undetectable. It brings one chosen card directly above the inserted card; the other directly beneath. The rest of the pack is spread out and drawn away, leaving only the three cards—two selected and one inserted between them.

The same trick can be performed with the aid of a knife, which is inserted instead of a face-up card. The procedure is exactly the same, the knife-blade serving as the indicator in this instance.

9. CARD IN CIGAR BOX A great trick. A chosen card is replaced in the pack, which the magician shuffles. The wizard then empties some cigars from an ordinary cigar box. He shows the box empty. He closes it and lays the pack on it. A mystic pass; the box is opened—the card is found therein.

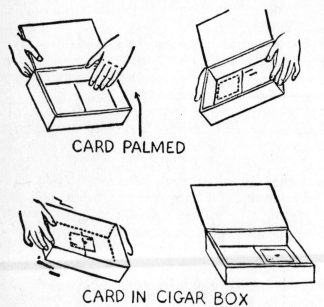

CARD PALMED

CARD IN CIGAR BOX

The diagrams illustrate the routine of the card in the cigar box.

The card actually goes into the cigar box—but before the spectators suppose. The magician gets it to the top of the pack. He palms it off and in going to the cigar box, keeps the card in readiness. The cigars are emptied—in drops the card from the wizard's palm.

The regulation cigar box is lined with paper—and the paper overlaps along the bottom. When the magician drops the card in the box, his hands are free and as he picks up the box to show it to the spectators, he tilts it so the selected card slides under the overlapping paper.

This enables him to show the box absolutely empty and to let the spectators close the box. When the box is shut, the magician sets it on the table, tilting it as he does so. The card drops from its hiding place. It is then in the box, ready for its mysterious appearance.

By using a duplicate card, the magician can have one already hidden in the box. He must then force that card upon the audience and later remove it from the pack.

10. CARD ELIMINATION   A card having been selected and returned to the pack, the magician offers to determine its identity by a process of elimination.

He takes eight cards and holds them faces down. Showing each card, he deals four on the table. None is the selected one. He deals two of these on the table. Neither is the one chosen. Then one card is left; it proves to be the chosen card.

This trick depends upon the sleight called the "glide."* The selected card is actually among the eight—which the magician does not show. The card is second from the bottom.

Here is the procedure: Holding the cards faces down, the magician shows the bottom card and asks if it is the chosen one. The spectator says that it is not. So the magician apparently deals it face down on the table. Actually he makes use of the "glide" and the chosen card is the one dealt.

The performer says he will put the next card back in the pack, eliminating it. So he draws off the bottom card of those in the little packet and replaces it on the pack without showing it. He shows the next card, however, and actually deals it

*Explained in Chapter Three.

face down. Then another on the pack, alternating thus, so there are four cards faces down on the table—the chosen card among them.

The magician gathers the four cards and sees to it that the selected card is again second from the bottom. He shows the bottom card and apparently deals it. Actually the chosen card is dealt—the "glide" again. The bottom card is then replaced, unshown, upon the pack. The next card is shown and dealt face down. The fourth goes into the pack.

The elimination has left only two cards—neither of which is supposed to be the chosen one. The spectators are wondering what the magician is about. He asks a person to place a hand on either card. Suppose the person touches the chosen card. The magician picks up the other card, shows its face and says: "Of course this is not your card," and replaces it in the pack. That leaves only one card. Turned up, it proves to be the chosen one.

Of course there is a possibility that the spectator will decide to touch the card which the magician wishes to eliminate. That makes no difference. He is simply told to turn up the card and look at it—not the chosen card, of course. It is put in the pack. That leaves just one card—which proves to be the chosen one.

Artfully done, this trick is surprising at the finish, because the performer seems to be dealing with cards other than the chosen one. The appearance of the selected card comes as a real bit of amazement. The trick must be done neatly—but very little skill is needed.

11. THE MAGNETIC CARD A very unusual method of discovering a chosen card. Holding the pack upright in his left hand, with the face of the pack toward the audience, the magician places his right forefinger upon the top of the pack, then slowly raises his right hand.

As though magnetized, a card rises with the forefinger until it is almost clear of the pack, when the performer catches it with his right hand and tosses it for inspection. It happens to be the chosen card.

To work this you must first bring the chosen card to the top of the pack, which will be the back of the pack as it is held in this instance. Hold the right hand with the thumb pointing up. Lay the forefinger on the top edge of the upright pack.

At the same time extend the little finger so that it lightly presses the rear of the pack. Now as you raise the right hand, the little finger slides the back card up, unseen. Noticing only the forefinger, the spectators are impressed by its magnetic power.

By previously moistening the tip of the little finger, the card can be carried clear of the pack, then lowered down into the center which the left hand holds loosely open for its reception—all apparently by the forefinger's magnetic attraction.

Chapter 6

CIGARETTE MAGIC

THIS CHAPTER COULD BE TITLED "TRICKS FOR THE Smoker" but the majority of its tricks are performed with unlighted cigarettes. Hence most of the items can be used by anyone on almost any occasion, rather than being restricted to a special field.

Being common articles (and easily borrowed!) cigarettes are excellently adapted to impromptu magic, which makes them very useful in connection with casual entertainment. They can be interspersed among other tricks of a similar nature, adding variety to the program.

A few of these cigarette tricks are of a more ambitious type, requiring a slight amount of preparation, but that makes them all the more effective. Always, the magician should convey the notion that simple articles could not be anything but ordinary, thus drawing attention from any thought of preparation.

1. THE BALANCED CIGARETTE Balancing one cigarette upright upon another is a very provoking proposition. It looks easy, but it just isn't. Hence when you do it and show how neatly it can be done, everyone will try to duplicate it, but without result.

There's a trick to it, hence your only problem is to conceal the fact. That pointed fact consists of an ordinary pin, which you previously push head first into one of the cigarettes. To make the cigarettes balance, you have only to set the one with the pin on top of the other, so that the pin point pushes down into the end of the lower cigarette.

It's simple to conceal the pin at the start by simply holding the cigarette at the end between your thumb and forefinger which continue to hide the pin while you are setting the cigarette upon the other.

At the finish of the balance, you can dispose of the pin as follows: assuming that the right hand is holding the lower cigarette, lift away the upper cigarette with the left hand and transfer it to the right, alongside the lower cigarette. Continuing downward, the left thumb and forefinger grip the pin and draw it away while the right hand is tossing the cigarettes on the table. The pin is dropped unnoticed to the floor.

Another method of balancing cigarettes is by using two cork-tipped cigarettes. Detach the cork-tip from a third cigarette and put it around the tip of one cigarette that you intend to use with the trick.

This extra tip should be slightly loose so it will slide, though not too easily. When you set one cigarette upon the other, use the cork-tipped ends. In adjusting the cigarettes, slide the loose tip slightly over the end of the other cigarette. This will lock the cigarettes sufficiently to balance them, if you handle the cigarettes steadily.

At the finish, the extra tip is drawn away by the left hand while the cigarettes are dropped on the table by the right.

2. CIGARETTE AND BOTTLE Presentation is an important factor in any trick and this particular trick offers great possibilities in that direction. Handled to the full degree, it can become a very uncanny stunt.

A cigarette is dropped into a small soda bottle. At the magician's command, the cigarette begins to rise and fall inside the empty bottle, finally climbing out through the neck and toppling clear.

The magician attributes all this to some weird, magnetic power, but the motivating force is actually a black thread and a pin, which preferably should be black too. Beforehand wind one end of the thread around the pin, near the head. Wind the other end of the thread around a button of the coat. Insert the pin into the end of a cigarette.

There should be about a foot of thread between the coat and the cigarette. Showing the cigarette, drop it into the bottle, pin end downward. The cigarette will fall to the bottom of the bottle and lie there, tilted upward.

Holding the bottle in the right hand, make mystic passes with the left. At the same time move the bottle forward and when the thread becomes taut, the cigarette will start to rise. When the process is reversed, the cigarette falls. All the while the left hand should act as though it were supplying the magnetic control.

Finally the left hand goes above the bottle and coaxes the cigarette right out. Timed to this maneuver the bottle is worked gradually forward to produce the result. The left hand catches the cigarette as it topples and you turn to set the bottle on the table with the right hand. At that moment, the left hand moves further away with the cigarette and the pin comes out when the end of the thread is reached.

The pin falls and dangles unnoticed on the end of the

thread, from which it can be detached later. That is why a black pin is preferable, particularly when working at close range, because it offers no visibility against a dark suit.

3. MUTUAL ATTRACTION Two cigarettes are placed on the table so that they lie parallel to the table edge, one cigarette being a few inches beyond the other. Announcing that the cigarettes have a mutual attraction, the magician takes the farther one between his thumb and finger and slides it slowly away from him to show that it will draw the other along.

At first the magnetism does not work, because it must be done at just the right speed and with the cigarettes at an exact distance apart. The magician leans forward to calculate this and at about the third attempt, the impossible happens. As the hand moves the farther cigarette toward the other side of the table, the closer cigarette rolls after it.

The secret is quite simple but highly deceptive when the trick is done neatly. In leaning forward, the magician blows on the table and thus causes the nearer cigarette to roll away from him. Since his head is tilted so he can gauge the distance, the magician can deliver the necessary breath undetected.

Also, in following the rolling cigarette with his eyes, the magician may raise his head sufficiently to continue the blowing process. All this must be timed to the action of the hand that is moving the decoy cigarette, hence the trick, though very easy, should be practiced to make it thoroughly effective.

4. THE PLIABLE CIGARETTE Quite a surprise, this trick, particularly suited to the casual performer since it has just the baffling touch needed for an impromptu mystery.

Borrowing a cigarette, the magician lights it, takes a few draws of smoke and then proceeds to bend the cigarette double, so that the two ends meet. Straightening the cigarette, the magician shows that it is quite intact and continues to smoke it.

Naturally, this intrigues the onlookers, but when they try the trick it won't work. Their cigarettes almost invariably break in half. But the magician can bend *any* cigarette, any time he wants (though he will do well to avoid cigarettes with cork tips), which only makes the mystery all the deeper.

The trick is practically done beforehand. Placing the cigarette in his mouth, the magician moistens its end well. Then while asking for a match or making some other comment, he removes the cigarette from his mouth. Before replacing the cigarette, the magician turns it around, so that his lips receive the other end—the dry end.

When the magician draws on the cigarette after lighting it, he pulls the moisture through the cigarette and gives it the flexibility needed to bend it in half without breaking.

5. MAGNETIZED CIGARETTES Several cigarettes are placed side by side on the outstretched right palm, being laid diagonally so they follow the line of the thumb and project slightly over the right side of the hand, between the thumb and fingers.

The left hand is set flat upon the cigarettes to hold them in place, while both hands are turned over, so that the cigarettes come beneath the right. The left hand is then removed and everyone expects to see the cigarettes fall.

Instead, the cigarettes remain there, held by some invisible attraction from the right palm. The projecting ends of the cigarettes can be seen below the right hand, but there is no explanation for their strange behavior. Finally the magician commands the cigarettes to fall and they drop to the table, where they may be examined, while the right hand is shown both empty and unprepared.

Here is the secret: In placing the left hand upon the cigarettes, lay it in the same diagonal direction as the cigarettes themselves. Bending slightly, the left hand can then secretly lift one of the cigarettes from the row.

Next, the left hand turns to criss-cross the right, the left fingers pointing to the base of the right thumb. This enables the left hand to plant its cigarette *across* the others and the

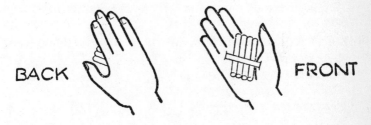

BACK   FRONT

right hand grips the stray cigarette between the base of the thumb and the little finger.

That is, the extra cigarette becomes a wedge, held by the right hand, keeping the remaining cigarettes in place against the right palm. The left hand presses the odd cigarette into position while the hands are slowly being turned over.

Now, when the left hand is removed, the cigarettes remain affixed to the right palm, with their projecting ends in sight, all except the end of the one cigarette which holds the others in position. The absence of one cigarette end will not be noticed, since four, five, or even six cigarettes are being used. Furthermore, the magician does not call attention to the original number and he keeps his right hand slightly in motion so that no one can count the extended ends.

The right hand must be a trifle cramped, but this does not matter, as people will still be puzzled at its ability to make so many cigarettes adhere to the hidden palm. However, the trick should be tested or practiced sufficiently beforehand, so that the hand's position will not appear too clumsy.

Before the spectators can guess what holds the cigarettes, the right hand is spread slightly, letting the cigarettes drop to the table. At the same time, the hand should make a slight twist or wave, which will cause the cigarettes to drop in scattered fashion, the odd cigarette falling among them. This disposes of the only clue, since there are nothing but cigarettes to be examined.

Some performers will find the trick easier with cigarettes of the long or "king size" variety. The trick may also be performed with large matches instead of cigarettes.

6. FIREPROOF NECKTIE Demonstrating that a necktie is fireproof is just another of the minor miracles with which magicians astound their friends. In this case, the demonstration is quite convincing, since it is done with a live cigarette.

Quite calmly, the magician lifts the end of someone's necktie and applies the lighted end of the cigarette to the cloth, holding it there firmly to give it a chance to burn. For a final convincer, the magician can press and twist the cigarette until its light is extinguished.

Then the ashes are brushed from the necktie and to the relief of the owner, it proves to be quite undamaged, thus bearing out the magician's claim that the necktie was fireproof. Only it wouldn't be fireproof if anyone but the magician put it to that test.

In his hand, the magician conceals a coin, either a quarter or half-dollar but preferably the latter. When he lifts the end of the necktie, he lets it lie flat across his fingers, with the coin hidden beneath it. In pressing the cigarette end against the necktie, the magician picks the exact spot where the coin is located.

The coin draws the heat through the cloth and thereby prevents the necktie from being burned, or even singed, provided the cloth is kept taut. Make sure however that the necktie has only a single thickness of cloth, otherwise the happy result is not guaranteed.

7. THE HYPNOTIC CIGARETTE PACK Taking a pack of cigarettes from his pocket, the magician extracts a cigarette then lays the pack on the edge of the table. Using the lone cigarette as a magnet to attract the pack, the magician accomplishes the impossible. He leaves the pack two-thirds extended over the edge of the table, yet it remains there unsupported, until he picks it up and pockets it.

Neither hypnotism nor magnetism are involved. Beforehand, remove the cigarettes from the pack, drop half a dozen pennies into the pack and replace the cigarettes. The bottom of the pack is the end that remains on the table; its added weight serves as the necessary counterbalance.

If cigarettes with cork tips are used, the magician can "explain" that cork is so light that the tips—toward the top of the pack—literally cause it to float in air. Also he can have another opened pack of cigarettes in his pocket, which he brings out later, so that other people can try the trick and fail.

With a new pack of cigarettes, three pennies can be slid under the paper wrapping at the bottom and used as the hidden counterbalance, but half a dozen coins inside a partly used pack will give the balance a longer range.

8. THREE ON A MATCH   Everyone is familiar with the old superstition of lighting three cigarettes on one match; how it is supposed to bring bad luck. Here the magician capitalizes on the ancient omen, proving that it won't work when he turns one match into three.

Striking a match, the magician gives it to someone, yet still has a lighted match in his own hand. He passes that match to a second person, but still retains a lighted match for himself. The thing happens so swiftly that the magician seems to be materializing matches from nowhere.

It's all done with a single paper match. Beforehand, split this match from the bottom to the head, separating the layers which form it. To all appearances it is an ordinary paper match, particularly when the thumb and forefinger press the separated layers together.

The match is struck and then the mystery begins. As soon as the head has burned, the one match is the equivalent of three. One layer or portion is handed to a person as though it were a single light, but the magician retains the rest. Handing the second segment to another person, the magician still has a "match" for himself, and a lighted match at that.

9. THE SURPRISING CIGARETTE   Here is a trick which is both perplexing and amusing and is particularly apt for the smoker. He takes a lighted cigarette from his mouth, turns the burning end toward his mouth and replaces the cigarette between his lips—but the lighted end is still away from the mouth!

When taking the cigarette from his mouth, the backs of his first and second fingers are placed against the lips, the thumb resting on his chin. The hand is then turned over so that the light really is toward the lips, but with his thumb, he pushes up on the cigarette giving it a second turn as the second finger moves away, which leaves the cigarette between the thumb and forefinger. The trick lies in the fact that two turns are made, not one as appears.

Chapter 7

EASY CARD TRICKS

THE TRICKS IN THIS SECTION CAN BE PERFORMED ANY-where at any time, with any pack of cards. They depend upon clever secrets or systems unknown to the spectators. None of them require any particular skill.

There are certain formulas in some of these tricks that will do the work, once the performer understands them. Each trick is a good one and an excellent program of card magic can be arranged from this section alone.

Practically every trick in this group is a mystery in itself, not depending upon any other method. Those persons already familiar with card magic will notice some novel ideas that may prove quite surprising to them. Certain principles have been adapted to new use and a close perusal of this section will prove of value to all card wizards.

1. CARD FOUND IN HAT Someone shuffles the pack and gives you half, keeping the other portion. Drop your half of the pack in a hat and begin to shake it; put another hat over the top so the shaking can be done very violently and the cards will be sure to mix.

After demonstrating this, let the spectator take three cards from his half and insert them one by one, face downward, between the brims of the hat. As each card comes in, you shake the hats to mix it with those that are already in. The spectator, of course, knows each card he pushes in between the hats.

After lots of shaking, you remove the upper hat and reach into the lower, producing the chosen cards one by one—much to the astonishment of the chooser.

It's all done when you put your cards in the hat. Give them a good bend at the center. Best, shake them first, showing how they mix. Then gather them into a pack again and bend this time, the hat covering the movement.

The selected cards mix with the others, right enough, but they are straight while the others are curved and it is easy to distinguish them. Then, in gathering the remaining cards from the hat, bend them the other way to straighten them and no clue remains.

2. TWO NUMBER TRICK   A pack is shuffled. Any person takes it and notes a card a certain distance from the top—not more than ten or twelve cards down.

Taking the pack, the magician holds it behind his back and asks another person to name a number above twelve. The magician promises to put the chosen card at the new number—even though he does not know the chosen card nor its position!

He apparently does this, for when the cards are counted, the chosen card is at the new number.

There is a point to this trick that most persons fail to grasp. That is the method of counting. It begins not at one, but at the mentally selected number.

To make this clear, let us consider the trick just as handled

99

by the performer. Suppose the fifth card is noted by the first party. Fifteen is the number named by the second person. Behind his back, the magician counts off fifteen cards, one by one, reversing their order. He drops them on top of the pack.

Giving the pack to the first spectator, he says: "Count to fifteen, starting the count with *your* number."

The person naturally counts: "Five, six, seven," and so on until he says "fifteen." He will then be at the card he chose. This trick always works, no matter what the two numbers may be. An interesting effect is to decide upon the higher number by using a pair of dice. Roll them often enough to get a total greater than twelve, adding the spots on each roll. Then proceed with the number thus determined.

3. BOTTOM TO TOP   This is a variation of the trick just described. It is given here as an alternate method. Many persons, seeing the two tricks, think that they are different in principle, whereas they are fundamentally the same.

Give the pack to a person. Tell him to pick any number less than ten and to remember the card that is that many from the bottom.

Take the pack and call for a number higher than ten. Suppose eighteen is given. Transfer eighteen cards from the bottom to the top, without changing their order. Move them in a group.

Now ask the first person's number. Suppose it is six. Counting from the top, begin with six. "Six, seven, eight—" a card for every number until you reach eighteen. That will be the card noted by the person as six from the bottom.

Let the man do the counting himself, if you wish, but always remember to have him start on his own number.

4. THOUGHT DISCOVERED The magician spreads a pack so that about ten or twelve cards in the center are visible when the front of the pack is elevated toward the onlookers. A spectator is requested to note one of the visible cards mentally and to write its name on a sheet of paper. The performer turns away while the name of the card is being written. The paper is folded and is given to another person. The magician shuffles the pack and gives it to the same person. The paper is then opened and the name of the mentally selected card is read. The person who has the pack looks through it for the chosen card. The card is missing—the magician immediately produces it from his pocket!

This is a very perplexing trick, yet it is not at all difficult. On the top of the pack the magician has ten or twelve cards that he has remembered, for instance: eight, queen, three, ten, two, seven, four, nine, king, ace.

This list, it will be noted, has no two cards of the same value, hence it is not necessary to remember suits. The magician may either arrange cards according to an order that he has previously memorized, or he can simply note the ten cards that happen to be duplicated in value. Most persons will prefer to set up the cards to conform with their regular arrangement, then there can be no mistake.

At any rate, the magician cuts the pack by drawing some cards from the bottom and putting them on top. He keeps the two sections of the pack slightly separated and spreads the center cards (those which were originally on top). Thus the spectator must think of one of those cards.

The writing of the card gives the performer an excuse to turn away. He immediately lifts the cards that are above the known group and puts them back on the bottom; that is, he simply shifts the original bottom half of the pack back to

101

where it belongs, so his ten known cards are again on top of the pack.

He then picks off at least ten cards and thrusts them in his pocket. One of those cards must be the one mentally selected.

When the slip of paper and the pack are handed to a spectator, the paper is naturally opened and read to learn the name of the missing card; while the spectator is looking for the card in the depleted pack, the magician simply puts his hand in his pocket and counts down to the required card. He, like the spectator, sees the name on the paper. Having his cards in a known order, he can easily find the right one. If the paper says "ten of spades," he counts eight, queen, three—*ten*.

He brings out the "missing" card and tosses it on the table, adding the additional cards to the pack at the first opportunity. The fact that the pack is depleted is never noticed.

5. TWENTY-FIVE CARDS A pack is shuffled. Five persons take five cards each. From his group, each person mentally selects a card. The magician gathers up the cards. He shows five cards and asks whose card is among them. A spectator says that he sees his card. The performer drops all cards but the chosen one. This is repeated until all five cards are discovered.

Here is the method: Let each person hold his group of five and remember one. He may shuffle his heap if he wishes. Go to the first person and ask for one card, face down. Then take a card from the second person, placing it on the card in your hand. Continue with persons three, four, five. Then go back to number one for another card.

You simply make the round, gathering cards one at a time until you have collected all twenty-five. But in this natural procedure, you have done something very important. You have arranged the cards in five groups: one, two, three, four, five—counting up from the bottom of the pack.

Now you take five cards from the top of those you hold. Fan them with the right hand. Although you alone know it, each of those cards has come from a different person. The card at the extreme left belongs to person one; the next to person two; three, four and five in order.

Show each person the fan. Ask if his card is there. If anyone says "yes," you immediately know which card it is, according to the person's number. Drop all cards but that one.

Now proceed with the next five cards. They will work just like the first five. Sometimes no one will have a card in the group. Just lay those cards aside. Sometimes two or three persons will see their card in the group. In that case drop one of the chosen cards, telling to whom it belongs; then drop the other and the third, if there is one.

You are not limited to twenty-five cards. You can use thirty-six if you wish, involving six persons in the trick. You can also use forty-nine cards, with seven persons.

6. A DOUBLE PREDICTION The magician takes twenty-one cards, among which is a conspicuous card—either the joker or the ace of spades. He writes two numbers—each on a separate slip of paper—without letting anyone see the numbers. He rolls up each piece of paper. Someone removes the joker from the packet of cards and shuffles the cards. The performer spreads the cards. The joker is pushed into the heap. One person is told to remember the card just above the joker; the other person remembers the card just below.

Squaring the cards, the magician deals them into two heaps. He spreads each heap separately, asking the persons to note their cards but to say nothing whatever. He places the heaps together and again deals two heaps, each of which is shown, but no comment is asked.

The heaps are placed together, the cards are spread and someone removes the joker. The packet is now cut into two heaps, one of which is counted, to make sure that there are at least eight cards in it.

Now the papers are opened. One bears the number 6—the other the number 4. The chosen cards are named. One is discovered six from the top in one heap; the other is found four from the top in the other heap!

Read the directions carefully. After the two cards have been noted, one on each side of the inserted joker, the joker is left in the pack and two heaps are dealt, one card at a time, alternately, reversing the order of the cards. Both heaps are spread and shown in turn. In putting them together, be sure that the heap of eleven cards goes on top of the heap of ten. Deal again—once more reversing the order of the cards—and show each heap. This time again be sure to place the heap of eleven on top of the heap of ten.

Now fan the cards with the faces toward the audience and ask a person to remove the joker. Here is the important part. When the joker is removed, one chosen card will be exactly five cards above that spot; the other chosen card will be exactly five cards below.

Cut the pack at the place from which the joker is removed. You will have one card five from the top—the other card five from the bottom. Square up the pack and cut it into two portions, as near equal as possible. Count the cards in the bottom section, reversing their order as you do so. Result: one chosen card is five from the top in one heap—the other is five from the top in the other heap.

In this explanation, it is assumed that the two numbers

written were 5 and 5—as that is the normal finish of the trick. But the reader will recall that in the description, we gave the numbers as 6 and 4. Certainly. They can be 6 and 4 just as well as 5 and 5. The crux lies in the cutting of the packet just after the removal of the joker. In cutting, draw one card from the top of the lower heap to the bottom of the upper, as you make the cut. Proceed just as with 5 and 5. But this time, the cards will turn up 6 and 4.

If you wish, you can make the cards come 7 and 3. This is done by drawing two cards from the top of the lower heap to the bottom of the upper as you make the cut. Now, if you prefer to have 8 and 2 as the final numbers, you can achieve that result by drawing three cards from the lower heap to the upper when you cut after the removal of the joker.

Of course you make up your mind what you are going to do before you start the trick. Then write the two numbers that you intend to use, each on a separate slip of paper. It is not wise to use 5 and 5, because the numbers are identical. 6 and 4 are better. But sometimes you may have to show the trick to people who have seen you do it before. So use 7 and 3 instead of 6 and 4.

Try this trick, using two conspicuous cards like red aces, one on each side of the joker. Go through the entire routine and you will then understand it. It is one of the best of all impromptu card tricks.

7. VANISHED CARD   Take a pack of cards and riffle the ends. Ask a person to think of any card that he sees. This is done. Again you riffle the pack. To the person's amazement, the card is gone—even though you riffle the pack slowly, he cannot see it.

The Secret: Divide the pack beforehand and carefully dovetail shuffle the two heaps together so that they alternate. In pressing the two sections together, do not shove them all the way. One group projects at one end, the other group at the other end.

When you riffle one end of the pack, only the projecting cards will show. Thus the spectator can select only from that

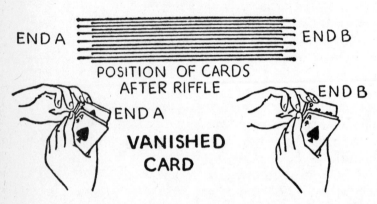

Note the projecting ends of cards and the method of riffling opposite ends of the pack.

group. To make his card disappear, simply turn the pack around and riffle the other end. His card will not come into view.

To make the trick doubly effective, riffle end A before a spectator and let him select a card. Riffle end B before another spectator and let him think of a card. Then riffle end B for spectator A. His card has vanished. Riffle end A for spectator B. His card is gone.

Ask the names of the cards. Press the projecting ends together, turn the pack over and run through the cards face up. Both vanished cards have returned.

8. THE REVERSING CARDS Showing a pack of cards, the magician riffles the ends, telling observers to notice the faces of the passing cards and notice that they are well mixed. Next, having shown that the faces are all different, he turns over the pack and riffles it to show the backs, which are all alike—as the backs of cards should be.

Then comes the surprise. Snapping one end of the pack and then the other, the magician spreads the pack along the table or from hand to hand and shows that a curious thing has happened. Half the cards have turned face upward in the pack, each face-up card being sandwiched between two face-downers and vice versa. That is, the cards of the entire pack are alternately face down and up!

This trick depends on the riffle principle, wherein the ends of the pack are not quite flush. Previously, divide the pack in half and turn one half up. Dovetail that half of the pack into the other; push the sections together but leave them projecting very slightly at the ends.

Riffle the pack from the proper end and people will see only faces, though half the cards are all that they actually view. Turn the pack over and riffle it to show the backs, which in turn will alone be seen. In snapping the ends of the pack, push the sections further in, so that the ends are flush.

Then spread the pack showing that every other card has turned face up, without a clue as to how the mystery was accomplished.

9. THE MYSTIC DISCOVERY This is an unusual idea in card magic—a trick that is very puzzling, yet which offers no great difficulties in presentation. It is a trick that must be thoroughly understood and which should be practiced to give it the neat precision which it requires. For the trick is most effective when done in an easy, efficient style.

The magician takes any pack after it has been shuffled. He holds it in his left hand and riffles the cards with his right, doing this slowly so that the spectators can see the faces of the cards as they fall.

"Think of any card that you see," says the magician. "If you note two or three, settle your mind upon one. You have it? Very well, I shall deal Bridge hands."

He then proceeds to deal the pack into four piles of thirteen each, which he designates as South, West, North and East. Picking up a hand, he spreads it and studies the cards for a moment. He turns the faces toward the person who chose the card.

"Is your card in this hand?" he asks.

If the reply is affirmative, the magician uses that heap; if negative, he shows the next hand—and so on, until he learns which pack contains the mentally selected card.

"That makes my chances a little better," says the magician. "I'm pretty sure I have your card. Our thoughts are working well."

He lays the heap face down upon the table and asks the spectator to name his card. The card is named. The magician turns up the top card of the pile and reveals the card that was mentally selected.

Now for the explanation. In riffling the cards, the magician begins while he is telling what he wants done. He does not turn the faces so they can be seen until he has run through about twenty cards rather rapidly—roughly, he has just about reached the center of the pack before the spectator has a real opportunity to glimpse the face of a card.

As the magician urges the person to think of a card, he lets the cards riffle slowly, one by one, allowing plenty of opportunity for the person to take any one of the cards that he sees. Approximately twelve cards are allowed to fall in this fashion; then, assuming that a card has been taken, the magician lets the rest of the cards riffle rapidly.

In brief, the wizard, despite the opportunity he seems to have given has actually limited the choice to one of a dozen cards, all located more than twenty from the bottom. When the heaps are dealt, there will be thirteen in each. They are dealt carefully; thus the bottom cards of the pack fall on top of the heaps.

Considering each heap individually, we can eliminate the top five cards and the bottom four. The selected card is sure to be either 6, 7, 8 and 9 from the top of its particular group. This is allowing sixteen cards—plenty of margin. But the magician wants an even better percentage. When he picks up one of the hands and spreads it, he is careful to keep the sixth and seventh cards out of sight behind the eighth. He allows a brief glance at the fan and asks if the spectator sees his card.

If the spectator sees his card in one of the heaps, the wizard knows that the card is either number eight or number nine from the top of the heap. Should the spectator fail to see his card in any hand, the explanation is obvious—to the magician only. He knows that the chosen card must be six or seven in its particular heap. So he chides the spectator for not looking closely enough and goes through the hands again. This time he spreads all of the cards—so the spectator naturally sees the chosen one. Thus the magician learns its heap.

Now for the finish. By the elimination process just described, the magician limits the chosen card to one of two—either six or seven in a certain heap; or eight or nine in that heap. He switches the cards around a bit and in the action

109

puts one of the possible cards on top of the heap; the other on the bottom. In a positive manner he lays the heap face down and calls for the name of the card. When it is given, the magician either turns up the top card or turns over the entire heap to show the bottom card—according to which one is named. Either revelation is surprising to the audience. Knowing the proper card, the magician simply uses the correct discovery.

10. THE SAME NUMBER Offer a pack to a person and ask him to shuffle it. Then tell him to count off any number of cards, while you are watching—at least ten cards—and to give you the remainder.

The person counts, say, sixteen. When you receive the balance of the pack, you ask him to lift his sixteen cards and drop them on. You hold the pack squared and show that all cards are even. Then, to demonstrate ease in counting, you lift off a bunch of cards and throw them on the table, announcing that you have taken sixteen. Counted, the statement proves correct.

It's all done when you receive the pack. Take the cards in the left hand, with the thumb across the back of the pack. Catch the ends of the pack with the right hand—thumb at one end and fingers at the other. Bend the ends up. When sixteen cards are put on the pack, square it and hold the cards tightly pressed. There is a space between the sixteen cards and the rest of the pack, but by pressing with the left thumb, you hide this fact.

Release pressure and the straight sixteen cards will rise, leaving the break below them. Simply lift off all cards above the break and throw them on the table. You have taken off the sixteen.

110

Shuffling the pack in dovetail fashion will destroy all traces of bent-up cards.

11. MATHEMATICAL DISCOVERY

Ask a person to think of a card. Tell him to remember its numerical value (ace, one; jack, eleven; queen, twelve; king, thirteen)—also the suit of the card.

Tell him to double the value of the card.

Then tell him to add three to the total.

Tell him to multiply the complete total by five.

This done, ask him to concentrate on the suit.

If the card is a diamond, he must add one.

If it is a club, he must add two.

If it is a heart, he must add three.

If it is a spade, he must add four.

He must then tell you the final total.

From it, you immediately divine the name of the selected card.

The secret is to subtract fifteen from the final total. You will have a number of two figures—possibly three. The last figure gives you the suit (diamonds 1, clubs 2, hearts 3, spades 4) while the first figure or figures give you the value.

Examples:

Jack of clubs.

11 doubled is 22. Add 3—25. Multiply by 5—125. Add 2 (for clubs) making 127. You are told that number.

Subtract 15 mentally. Result, 112. Last figure (2) means clubs. First figures (11) mean jack.

With the five of hearts.

5 doubled is 10. Add 3—13. Multiply by 5—65. Add 3 (for hearts) making 68. You are told that number.

Subtract 15 mentally. Result, 53. Last figure (3) means hearts. First figure (5) means five spot.

This is a very effective routine and it is particularly valuable when a troublesome spectator takes a card and makes it impossible for you to go ahead with the trick as you have intended it.

Remember that the spectator performs all his calculation without telling you a word about the card itself. He can do it mentally or on paper. All you ask is the total. The total does not appear to give you any clue to the card, because no one knows your secret system of deducting 15.

12. THREE HEAPS   A spectator deals three cards faces up. He counts the value of one card and turns it down. He adds enough cards to it to make fifteen. For example, if the card is a seven, he deals eight cards on it.

He repeats this process with the other two cards. Then the magician comes in and takes the cards that remain. He quickly tells the total value of the three cards on the bottoms.

The system is this: Count the cards that remain. Disregard four of them. The rest will be the same as the total of the hidden cards.

Face cards are usually counted as ten in this trick. If desired, jack can be eleven; queen twelve; king, thirteen. It makes no difference.

While the trick is very bewildering to those who do not understand it, it is readily understood if we consider it with three aces as the bottom cards. That means fifteen cards in each heap. The total is forty-five. That leaves seven cards over. The total of the aces is three. So four cards must be disregarded.

112

Now, if a two-spot is put in place of one of the aces, the total of the bottom cards becomes five instead of four. But the use of a two-spot means one less card in that heap, one card more in the surplus. Hence the rule works, no matter what the value of the base cards may be.

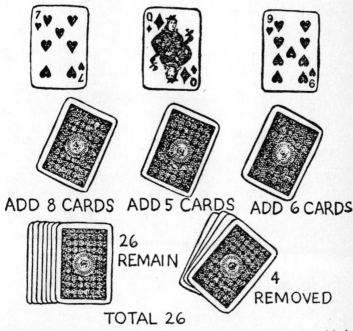

ADD 8 CARDS   ADD 5 CARDS   ADD 6 CARDS

26 REMAIN

4 REMOVED

TOTAL 26

Typical layout of three heaps, with additional cards added to make totals of fifteen.

13. MANY HEAPS   This effect is similar to the three heap trick; but in this instance the face cards must count as ten and after a card is placed on the table, other cards are added to make the total twelve.

For instance, a seven is laid face down. That means five

cards must be dealt on it. If a king is laid face down, two cards must be added.

There is no set limit to the number of heaps. The dealer may use three as in the other trick; but he may use more—

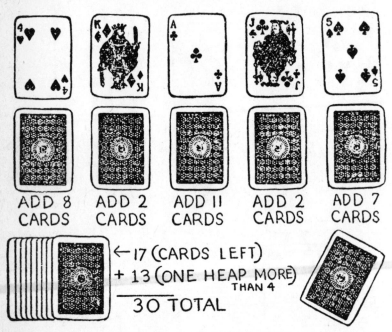

ADD 8 CARDS   ADD 2 CARDS   ADD 11 CARDS   ADD 2 CARDS   ADD 7 CARDS

←17 (CARDS LEFT)
+ 13 (ONE HEAP MORE)
       THAN 4
 30 TOTAL

Typical layout of five heaps, indicating additional cards making totals of twelve.

five, six, or seven—in fact, he may continue until he has no more cards to make up totals.

The performer recommends that at least five heaps be used, if possible. When he returns, he takes the extra cards, looks at the heaps, and names the total of the bottom cards.

To understand this, let us consider it with four heaps. Four

114

aces on the bottoms mean forty-eight cards used. There will be four cards left over. That is the total. In other words, with four heaps in use, the extra cards tell the total exactly.

Now when the performer returns, he counts the extra cards and disregards four of the heaps. For each additional heap, he simply adds thirteen. Why? Because if we had four kings as bottom cards, with two cards on each, there would be a total of forty extra cards. Now the formation of a fifth heap with an ace on the bottom would require twelve of those forty cards. It would also add one to the total of the under cards. That means thirteen.

Thus if we have six heaps and twelve cards left over, the total of the under cards will be 13 plus 13 plus 6, or 32. With seven heaps and nine cards over, the total will be 13 plus 13 plus 13 plus 9, or 48.

If a spectator decides to use only three heaps, simply subtract thirteen from the total number of cards left over. If he uses only two heaps, subtract twenty-six from the remaining cards.

Four heaps is the basis of the formula and there is no difficulty whatever in determining the totals. The trick is a good one to repeat, because the spectators will try varied numbers of heaps and will find this experiment more perplexing as it continues.

Chapter 8

DIVINATION TRICKS

Under this one head are found a variety of tricks that all aim toward the same objective: namely, to prove that the magician has some peculiar ability at discovering things which have happened outside his normal range of knowledge.

To the audience, some of these tricks will appear very much alike; from the magician's standpoint they are decidedly different, since he considers them from the processes involved. This will give the reader an insight into the contrast between "effect" and "method," the two terms which respectively define a trick from the opposite views of spectator and magician.

In all magical performances, the effects should be diversified, otherwise the program may become monotonous. Hence although the tricks in this chapter are grouped together, it is not advisable to perform too many of them on one occasion. The grouping, in this case, is for the benefit of the reader so that he may have a choice of the numerous methods and gain a working knowledge of all.

Nevertheless there is a certain value in repetition of effects, particularly where Divination Tricks are concerned. People often want to see a trick again and where the magician is putting across the idea of some unusual ability—as divination

—he cannot well refuse. That is when the knowledge of extra and alternate methods will come in handily.

1. DOLLAR DIVINATION Several dollar bills are used in this effect. Someone is asked to pick one of the bills and write down its serial number so that it can be identified later. The magician then rolls the bill into a tight wad, so that only the green side shows and therefore the number can not be seen.

Dropping the wadded bill into a hat, the magician tells the spectator to wad the other bills in exactly the same way and throw them into the hat with the first one. The hat is given a thorough shake; the magician reaches into the hat, brings out a bill. When the magician opens the bill and hands it to the person, it is found to be the bill with the listed serial number.

It all happens when the magician is wadding the chosen bill. Concealed in his hand, the magician holds a fair-sized glass bead. As he crumples the bill, he lets the bead drop inside it. The other bills are wadded to resemble the chosen one, but they all lack the bead that provides an added weight. From the hat, the magician easily brings the chosen bill, finding it because it is heavier. In unrolling the bill, he lets the hidden bead drop back into his hand.

A metal ball-bearing, if available, is better than a bead because it is heavier. Also the trick may be done with squares of thin paper, each bearing a crayon mark of a different color in the center. In this case, the magician picks a chosen color instead of a bill number.

2. FIND THE PENCIL The performer turns his back and puts on a blindfold while several pencils are borrowed from the spectators and put into a hat. One is then removed and passed from person to person to "create a magnetic force." It is then dropped into the hat with the others.

The performer then takes one pencil at a time and holds it to his forehead. He then announces the pencil which was selected.

The secret of this is a confederate who places a small dab of cold cream on the chosen pencil when he handles it. Ordinarily, he is the last to touch it, but the dab is so tiny, it would pass unnoticed even if handled by another spectator.

The performer slides his fingers from the center to the ends of each pencil and detects the chosen pencil by the bit of cream, which is what he has been looking for. The cream is removed and its presence will not be detected when the pencil is returned to the spectator from whom it was borrowed.

3. THE FAVORITE BRAND Blindfold tests with cigarettes form the basis for this feat in divination magic. However, a magician does not have to smoke a cigarette in order to tell the kind it is. He does it the hard way, dropping several borrowed cigarettes into a hat, then reaching in and picking out the one he wants. This happens either while the magician is blindfolded or the hat is held above the level of his head.

Start the trick by asking which brand the audience wants you to pick. Borrowing a cigarette of that brand, you drop it in the hat, then gather others, but all of other brands and toss these into the hat too. Naturally, you look at the cigarettes as you toss them into the hat, so you are sure that there is only one of the particular brand you are supposed to find. The hat may be shaken before you proceed to pick out the right cigarette.

It is the slight handling of the cigarettes that enables you to do the tricks. As you receive the cigarette of the favorite brand and announce you will drop it in the hat, hold it at the center between your thumb and second finger. Press the cigarette and roll it between thumb and finger as you reach for the hat.

This softens the center of the cigarette and makes it easy to distinguish from the others that you toss in with it. Simply feel for the cigarette with the weak center and pick it out.

4. MOVE THE CIGARETTES A dozen or more cigarettes are laid in a row on the table and a person is invited to move some of the cigarettes from the left end of the row to the right. He is to remember the number moved and he can slide the cigarettes slightly to the left, so the row will be in approximately its original position, thus giving no clue to the number moved.

This is done while the magician's back is turned. Not until the spectator has moved the number he wants does the magician look at the row. Then, running his hands along the row of cigarettes, the magician gains a mental impression and promptly states the number moved. The trick may then be repeated.

The magician should use his own cigarettes for this trick, as it requires a special type of brand, the sort that have the name printed along the side of the cigarette at the center. In laying the cigarettes on the table, the magician sees to it that all the names run in the same direction with one exception.

That is the "key" cigarette. The magician remembers its position in the row, say third from the right. After some cigarettes have been moved, the magician notes the new position of the "key" and subtracts the old number. For instance if the "key" winds up ninth from the right, the magician knows that six cigarettes were moved, since the original position was three.

Brands bearing names at the end can be used, provided the printing is light or inconspicuous. In this case, one of the cigarettes is turned opposite the others, to serve as the "key."

5. WITH SUGAR LUMPS The magician places four or five lumps of sugar upon the table. He pushes them around a bit, changing their position, and invites spectators to do the same.

He states that he will turn his back and that while he is looking the other way, the spectators are to choose one lump of sugar. Someone is to pick up that lump and hold it to his forehead, then replace it on the table with the others.

The magician turns his back, the lump of sugar is selected and lifted from the table, then replaced. When all is ready, the magician turns around. He picks up each lump in turn, holds it to his forehead in order to gain the correct impression. When he comes to the chosen piece of sugar, he announces it.

A slight preparation is necessary, and it depends upon another dinner table material other than the lumps of sugar. The needed item is salt.

Lay the lumps of sugar near you, some time before the trick is performed. Upon each lump, place a small pinch of salt. The sugar is white; so is the salt. Hence the salt cannot be noticed.

When you explain the purpose of the trick, you push the lumps of sugar around the table and specify that only the chosen one must be lifted. Your reason for this is that you depend upon a "magnetic" impression. Actually, you are seeing to it that the lumps of sugar do not lose their loads of salt.

After your back is turned, someone lifts a lump of sugar.

120

The salt falls off. Since the quantity is small, this will not be noticed. Upon the white table cloth, the grains will lie unobserved.

When the lump is replaced and pushed about with the others, you return and pick up the bits of sugar, one by one. It is not necessary to look for the salt that each lump carries. By placing your thumb on top of each lump when you lift it, you feel the salt, like a tiny cushion.

One lump will have no salt. Your thumb will sense that fact immediately. The absence of the salt tells you that the lump of sugar is the chosen one.

6. PICK THE PACK The magician shows some packs of paper matches, each of a different pattern. He lays them on the table—asks someone to choose any match pack and open it while the magician's back is turned. The person can remove a match if he wishes. Whether he does or not, he is to close the pack and replace it with the others. They are then handed to the magician.

Holding each pack to his forehead, one by one, the magician finally selects one and tosses it on the table. The pack that the magician picks is the one that the spectators chose.

You take each pack that you intend to use and open it, to show the matches inside. When you close the pack, press its cover firmly with your thumb, thus wedging the loose flap tightly shut. This slight action is not noticeable as you keep your thumb away from view.

When a person opens the selected match pack, he unwittingly loosens the tight flap. Closing the pack in normal fashion, he fails to wedge the flap like the others. When you receive the packs and hold them to your forehead, you keep the flap sides toward you and test them with pressure of your thumb. The one that opens without pressure is the chosen one.

7. COLORED CRAYONS Several colored crayons are used in this feat of divination. While the magician's back is turned, a crayon is dropped in his hand. He then turns, faces the spectators and concentrates, saying he will try to guess the color. To help the mental process, the magician holds one hand to his forehead, still keeping the crayon behind his back.

After a few moments, the magician names the color, and correctly. He turns around, lets a spectator reclaim the crayon, and proceeds to repeat the trick with another crayon.

The crux comes when the magician faces the audience. At that point, his hands are busy behind his back. With his left hand, the magician marks his right thumb-nail with the crayon. Retaining the crayon in his left hand, the mental master raises his right hand to his forehead, spots the color on this thumb-nail and has the answer.

This trick can be made more effective by using a small tube with a cover, large enough to hold a crayon conveniently. In this case, the spectator puts his crayon into the tube and hands it to the wizard. The process is the same, except that behind his back, the magician must open the tube, slide the crayon part way out to make the thumb-nail mark. After that he caps the tube as before.

8. NAME THE FLAVOR Performed with packages of candy drops this divination effect has a very tasty touch. The magician uses four packages of candy drops, representing such flavors as lemon, lime, orange and raspberry. These packages, which come in the shape of tubes, are identical except for their labels and of course the contents, which are sealed.

Behind his back the magician receives one of the packages, then faces the audience and goes into the usual concentration after which he names the flavor of the particular pack which he is holding behind his back.

The packages are prepared beforehand but in a subtle way that will not be detected. Such packages have labelled wrappers which slide off like outer tubes. Slide off three of these beforehand and prepare the contents as follows:

For lemon, break the package at the center.
For lime, break the package near one end.
For orange, break the package near both ends.
For raspberry, leave the package intact.

Receiving a package behind your back, you have only to slide off the label and you can tell by the breaks (or their absence) which flavor the package contains.

Of course in doing the trick, you pass around the packages with their wrappings on them as they were originally. After testing a package behind your back, you again slide its wrapper over it. For a finish, break open the packages and pass the candy around. That settles all the evidence.

9. RIBBONS AND PINS The magician shows four safety pins all alike. The pins are clasped and each has a tiny bit of ribbon attached to it. The ribbons are of different colors.

One of these pins is given to the magician, behind his back. He immediately names the color of its ribbon.

First, dull the points of two safety pins with a file or by rubbing them against a stone. Then attach the ribbons to each pin, according to the following arrangement:

1) Red ribbon. On solid bar of a dull pin.
2) White ribbon. On solid bar of a sharp pin.

3) *Green ribbon. On loose bar of a dull pin.*
4) *Blue ribbon. On loose bar of a sharp pin.*

To learn the color of any ribbon, simply open the pin and find whether its point is sharp or dull. Note also if the ribbon is tied to the loose bar or the solid. These two clues give you the color of the ribbon.

10. DIVINING THE COLORS

10. DIVINING THE COLORS With several skeins of different colored yarns, this trick will prove an experiment in telepathy.

The magician turns his back and one of the skeins is placed in his hand. Holding his hands behind his back, he turns to face the spectator and concentrates for a few seconds. He reverses his position again and the yarn is still in his hand, but he instantly names the color.

The Method: When the magician faces his audience after receiving the yarn, he breaks off a bit of the yarn and holds it behind his back. He retains the original yarn in the hand behind his back, but the tiny sample is in the other, and when he raises his hand to his forehead in concentration, he sees the color, turns and names the color.

11. CARDS AND ENVELOPES

11. CARDS AND ENVELOPES Four colored cards are used in this trick, along with four envelopes, preferably of the "pay-envelope" type, which opens at the top.

Spectators place the cards in different envelopes; the envelopes are shuffled about and handed to the magician. Holding each envelope to his head he identifies the color of the card that it contains.

Some minor preparation is required in this trick. In preparing the cards, which can be cut from thin, colored cardboard, gauge them very carefully and make them slightly different sizes. One card, which serves as a standard, should be cut so it fits snugly into an envelope. Assuming this to be a red card, the cards can be prepared as follows:

Red: Standard size, tight fit.

Yellow: Cut slightly narrow.

Green: Cut slightly short.

Blue: Cut narrow and short.

Though the difference in sizes should not be noticeable to sight, when the cards are in the envelopes, you can detect them by squeezing the sides of the envelope with one hand, then transferring it to the other hand and squeezing the ends. Any "give" in either instance will be your clue to the color of the card inside the envelope.

12. SIX BOTTLE CHOICE   Six bottles are placed upon the table. Each is identified by a gummed label. The bottles are numbered from 1 to 6. There is a seventh bottle—unnumbered—which is filled with liquid.

The magician requests a spectator to pour some of the liquid into any one of the six bottles that he chooses. Having done this, the unnumbered bottle, which contained the liquid, is sent out to the medium.

After receiving the bottle which was used in *pouring,* the medium gives the number of the bottle into which the liquid *was poured!*

In preparing for this trick, you must first arrange the corks of the six numbered bottles. Each of these must be marked to indicate its bottle. It is best to mark the under side of each cork. One, two or three dots in the center indicate bottles 1, 2 and 3. One, two or three dots near the edge indicate bottles 4, 5 and 6.

In presenting the trick, pick up the bottle with the liquid, remove its cork and give the bottle to a spectator, setting the cork on the table. Ask him to choose any one of the six bottles. When he does so, pick up the empty bottle—say number 3—and remove its cork. Let him pour liquid into bottle 3.

Immediately pick up the cork which you took from the *full bottle* and use it to cork *bottle 3*. Point to the cork on the table and tell the spectator to replace the cork in the bottle from which he poured the liquid.

Subtly, you have *exchanged corks*. Thus when your medium, stationed in another room, receives the bottle from which the liquid was taken, he learns, by examining the cork, the number of the bottle into which the liquid was poured.

Chapter 9

SPELLING TRICKS

SPELLING TRICKS ARE A FORM OF CARD MAGIC THAT CAME into popularity years ago and have been elaborated into a branch of trickery all their own. While they come under the head of Card Discoveries, most "Spellers" are complete tricks in themselves, which helps render their performance more effective.

Fundamentally, a "Speller" consists in having a person name a chosen card, whereupon the magician begins to "spell" cards from the pack, dealing cards along with each letter. At the conclusion of the trick, the spelling process discovers the chosen card.

This in itself is an intriguing finish to any card trick, which is why the "Spellers" sprang into favor so rapidly. But these tricks also offer application of clever and unusual methods which would not be possible with the average card trick Therefore they deserve their own chapter in this book.

Some tricks suffer from repetition, but Spelling Tricks are just the reverse. Because they have so many variants, they grow more perplexing as they go along, and can be interspersed through a card routine with excellent results.

1. SIMPLICITY SPELLER The magician takes a pack of cards and spreads it between his hands, running the cards from left to right. He asks a person to select a card and to remove it from the pack. That having been done, the magician lifts some cards so that the chosen one may be replaced.

Riffling the pack, the magician states that he will make the card choose its own position. He asks the spectator to name the card. We will suppose that it is the five of hearts. The magician commences to deal the cards, spelling: "F-I-V-E-O-F-H-E-A-R-T-S"—a letter for each card. With the final "S", he turns up the card. It proves to be the five of hearts.

In running the cards from the left hand to the right, the magician counts them. He does not give anyone a chance to take a card until he has run eleven cards along the fan. He pushes the cards more slowly after the eleventh, keeping a slight space between the eleventh card and the twelfth.

When a card is removed, the magician invites its replacement, by lifting the eleven cards at the top of the pack. As a result, the selected card takes the position of number twelve.

Now it is not at all difficult to spell to the chosen card after it is named. Simply count the letters to one's self. If the card is spelled with eleven letters, spell it and turn up the twelfth. If twelve letters, end the spelling on the twelfth. With thirteen letters, leave out the word "O-F".

Example:
Queen of Hearts.
Spell: "Q-U-E-E-N-H-E-A-R-T-S" and turn up the next card. With fourteen letters, leave out the word "O-F" and turn up the card with the final letter of the spelling.

With a ten-letter card, the magician turns the top card of the pack face up and appears surprised because it is not the chosen card. He pushes that card into the middle of the pack; then spells the name of the selected card, turning up the card after the last letter.

With a fifteen-letter card, the magician spells very slowly. He says, for example: "Your card was the seven of diamonds? I shall spell 'S-E-V-E-N'. The suit? A diamond? Very well: 'D-I-A-M-O-N-D'."

He turns up the card on the final "D" and reveals it as the seven of diamonds. Thus by a little ingenuity, the chosen card can be spelled every time. This is one of the most practical and effective versions of the spelling trick. It requires some amount of rehearsal in order to be presented convincingly, but the skill involved is negligible.

2. SPREAD-OUT SPELLER A shuffled pack is spread along the table. A card is chosen from any spot. Only the person selecting it sees it. The card is replaced from where it

SPREAD OUT SPELLER

Noting thirteen cards above selected one. Making break at that point. Shifting extra cards to bottom. Also the final position.

was taken. The performer picks up the pack and requests the name of the card. He spells the name, dealing a card with each letter. The spelling ends by the turning up of the chosen card.

It is all a matter of careful counting. The pack is spread clear along the table. As soon as the spectator touches a card, the magician counts along the line to a spot thirteen cards above the chosen one (beginning the count with the touched card).

As the spectator replaces the card he took, the magician still keeps his eye upon the place to which he has counted. He has spread the cards from left to right. Sliding them up with his left hand, he holds a break with his left thumb when he reaches the spot to which he has counted. The right hand simply transfers all cards above the break, putting them on the bottom of the pack.

Thus the chosen card is thirteen from the top. The wizard asks its name and spells in such a manner that he ends with the chosen card.

For instance, if the card has only ten letters, he adds the word "T-H-E" before it. Example: "T-H-E-A-C-E-O-F-C-L-U-B-S". With eleven letters, he removes the top card from the pack, strikes the pack with it, and thrusts the card into the pack at the center. This by-play disposes of an odd card. It leaves only twelve to deal. The magician spells with eleven cards and turns up the *next* card.

Twelve letters is a simple spelling, turning up the next card; thirteen letters spells right to the card itself. With fourteen letters, eliminate the word "O-F" and turn up the card after the spelling. With fifteen letters, eliminate "O-F" and turn up on the final letter.

There is another method of gathering up the cards from the table—simply a variation of the one described. Sweep

130

them up with the right hand until the desired spot is reached. Then transfer those cards to the left hand and use them as a lever to gather up the cards from left to right. This puts the chosen card thirteen from the top.

3. FOUR HEAP SPELLER This is one of the most interesting versions of the spelling trick. It can be demonstrated with an ease of action that defies detection. It requires boldness more than skill.

A spectator is asked to shuffle a pack of cards and to cut it in half. He is then requested to cut each half into two equal portions. The result: four heaps.

He is told to look at the top card of any heap and to place it on any other heap. This done, the magician gathers the heaps, burying the chosen card in the pack.

The card is named. The magician proceeds to deal cards off, faces upward, spelling a letter as he deals each card. "F-O-U-R-O-F-H-EA-R-T-S"—he spells, and on the letter "S" he is holding the four of hearts!

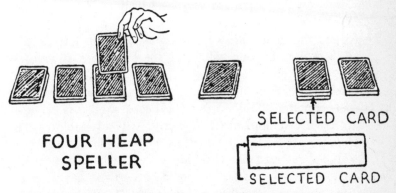

FOUR HEAP
SPELLER

SELECTED CARD

SELECTED CARD

Left: Division of pack in four equal heaps. Right: One heap placed on selected card. Final position before the spelling.

It so happens that the separation of the pack into four approximately equal heaps puts about thirteen cards in each heap. Thus, when a card is selected from the top of a heap, it is quite possible to put that card just about thirteen from the top when the heaps are gathered. Merely drop a single heap upon the chosen card.

Let us suppose, by way of example, that the chosen card is just about thirteen from the top of the pack—the exact location being unknown. When the cards are spelled, they are dropped faces up, each letter being given just before the card is tilted into view.

The count, or spelling, is rapid at first, but it slows appreciably. "F-O-U-R-O-F-D-I---A---M---O---N---D---". On the final "D", we have reached the zone of the selected card. If it turns up on the letter "D", the magician smiles and holds the card out for all to see. He has completed the spelling! If it does not show up, he drops the card; then, he deals another card saying "S". This is likely to be the chosen card—if so, the trick is done. If it is not the chosen card, he simply drops it and deals off the *next* card very decisively, turning it up to reveal it as the four of diamonds.

In brief, the magician has *three chances* of hitting the chosen card and any one will bring the trick to a successful finish.

It is wise, in picking up the heaps, to drop a slightly undersized heap on the chosen card. The heaps should be almost equal. They are seldom exact, however. It is advisable to put *ten* or *eleven* cards on top, in preference to a larger number.

The magician must act carefully when he begins to spell. With any ten-letter card, such as the ace, two, six, nine of clubs, he does best to spell with the word "T-H-E" leading off, giving the particular card a thirteen valuation. With any fif-

132

teen-letter card, such as the three, seven, eight, queen of diamonds, he should spell simply the value and the suit, eliminating the word "O-F".

By following this plan, the performer is almost certain of striking the chosen card on one of his three all-important chances. With a reasonable amount of rehearsal, the trick becomes almost certain of success. The performer may, if he wishes, form the four heaps himself, thus increasing the chances of exactness.

4. THE MENTAL SPELLER The magician takes a pack of cards and opens it some distance from the top, spreading a series of cards so that they come into view when the front of the pack is fanned before a spectator's eyes.

The onlooker is told to make a mental selection of any card. The wizard closes the pack and riffles it. He asks the name of the card. Whatever it may be, the magician promptly spells to the chosen card. He may then repeat the trick with another person.

The secret lies in the special arrangement of seven cards. It will be noted that each of these cards is spelled with a different number of letters; the sixth and seventh are the same, but there is a simple way of giving an extra value to the seventh.

S-I-X O-F C-L-U-B-S . . . . 10 letters

A-C-E O-F H-E-A-R-T-S . . . . . . 11 letters

Q-U-E-E-N O-F C-L-U-B-S . . . . . 12 letters

E-I-G-H-T O-F S-P-A-D-E-S . . . . . 13 letters

K-I-N-G O-F D-I-A-M-O-N-D-S . . . . 14 letters

S-E-V-E-N O-F D-I-A-M-O-N-D-S . . . . 15 letters

T-H-R-E-E O-F D-I-A-M-O-N-D-S* . . . . 16 letters

133

The asterisk (*) indicates that a card is turned up *after* the spelling is completed. In the other instances, the spelling ends with the final letter in the name of the card.

Based on this simple formula, the magician is ready to mystify. He arranges his seven pet cards and places nine indifferent cards upon them. The entire group goes on top of the deck. Performing, the magician casually counts nine cards down and spreads the pack at that point, so when he turns the faces toward the audience. only seven cards are in view— the seven arranged cards.

It makes no difference which one is selected. The magician simply spells to it. Ten spelled letters arrive on the six of clubs; eleven on the ace of hearts; and so on—the only special instance being the three of diamonds. If it is the chosen card, the magician spells his deal and turns up the next card after he has completed.

Of course the trick can be repeated. This can be done with the same set-up. It is an excellent idea, however, to have another group of cards arranged. Place nine indifferent cards under the three of diamonds; then set: ten of clubs, two of spades, seven of clubs, queen of hearts, jack of diamonds, three of diamonds, queen of diamonds.

After spelling to the chosen card of the first group, casually drop those cards aside; also the few more that may remain in the group. Again bunch nine cards at the top of the pack and give selection of the second set-up.

It is merely a repetition of the trick. When only one group is being used, any borrowed pack may be quickly arranged as there are various options: ace of spades will answer for ten of hearts; three of spades for eight of spades, etc.

This cannot be regarded as a trick with a prearranged pack because the actual preparation is such a simple matter and may often be done in the course of other tricks. Even if the magician should pick his own cards, and someone comment upon the fact, he can easily explain it as a problem of psychology, stating that he will cause a person to pick a certain card, even against his will.

The "Mental Speller" is quite different from most of the other spelling effects and forms an excellent variation that will create much favorable comment among those who witness its performance.

5. THE PROGRESSIVE SPELLER   This form of the spelling trick requires some arrangement of the cards. That, however, should not detract from the effect, especially when the trick is presented at a small gathering where the magician appears as a special performer.

Several persons are handed packets of cards. Each is told to remember one card. The magician gathers each packet. He places all on the pack. He calls upon one spectator to name his card. This done, the magician spells to the card exactly. The effect is repeated with each of the other persons.

We have stated that "several" persons are handed "packets" of cards. In practice, the number of persons is exactly four; and there are just five cards in each heap. These cards are arranged progressively for spelling, as in the "Mental Speller."

Group 1: jack of clubs, four of hearts, queen of spades, five of diamonds, eight of diamonds.

Group 2: ten of hearts, eight of clubs, seven of spades, jack of diamonds, seven of diamonds.

Group 3: two of spades, queen of clubs, ten of diamonds, king of diamonds, three of diamonds.

Group 4: ace of hearts, king of spades, eight of hearts, four of diamonds, queen of diamonds.

These heaps are on top of the pack. If the magician indulges in cuts or shuffles before dealing, he must use false ones that do not disturb the order of the twenty cards. He goes to four different persons, dealing five to each in turn. He fans the cards for a selection and has the person hold his cards just as given to him—face down, after the mental selection.

Finishing with the four persons, the magician casually counts off two more groups of five, both as one, while he is talking. He is about to move to another person when he decides that four are enough. Holding the ten extra cards in his right hand, he presents the pack so that each person holding five can replace his group of cards. The magician remembers the order of the persons as they return their packets.

Noting the cards in his right hand, he throws them on the pack and gives the pack a riffle or a false cut. He calls upon the last person who returned the packet to name his chosen card. Given, the performer spells to it. The presence of the ten cards on top enables the magician to spell exactly to the mentally selected card, no matter which one of the five happened to be taken.

All dealt cards are immediately put back on the pack. The magician picks off the top five, fans them and reminds his audience that the selected card was chosen mentally from a group. He slides the five fanned cards to the bottom of the pack. He is now set to spell the card chosen by the third replacer, as he has ten indifferent cards upon that particular person's packet.

Repeating his previous maneuver, so as to replace ten cards, the magician spells the second replacer's card; and finally the first man's card.

This trick will be readily understood by experiment with actual cards and the magician who uses it will find that it can be worked up to an excellent effect. It may be improved or varied by the use of a few false shuffles and great importance should be laid upon the fact that each chooser takes his card mentally from a group.

This trick is suitable for presentation with giant cards and should make a very fine showing on a small platform or stage. It is not essential to place the cards in the spectators' hands, although that facilitates matters when working with cards of ordinary size, at close range.

6. A SPELLING TRICK The performer offers to show just how the cards tell their own story. He takes a pack from his pocket and deals the cards faces down, one by one, spelling: "A-C-E—" turning up the third card to lay it aside. It is an ace. Continuing, he spells "T-W-O"—turning up a card and laying it aside on the letter "O". It is a two. He continues thus, turning up a three, a four, and so on. With "J-A-C-K—" he turns up a jack. With "Q-U-E-E-N—" a queen; and on the last letter—the "G" of "K-I-N-G"—he turns up a king, the final card of the pack!

Now for the addition. Thirteen cards are lying faces up, in order from ace up to king. The rest of the pack is back up, the cards together as they have been dealt one on the other. Picking up the face-up cards, the magician turns them face down and lays the packet on the other cards. He remarks that he has spelled values; he will now spell suits also.

"Take a king," he says. "The highest card—and hearts as a suit."

He deals the cards face down, spelling "K-I-N-G—O-F—H-E-A-R-T-S". He turns up the *next* card. It is the king of hearts.

"There are four suits," says the magician. "Four from king

137

is nine. We have hearts; let's try diamonds—the nine of diamonds."

He spells the name of the card, dealing with it. He turns up the next card after the spelling. It is the nine of diamonds.

"Now for the blacks. Four from nine is five. We'll aim for the five of clubs."

The spelling follows. Right after the "S" the magician turns up the five of clubs.

"We have one more suit—spades. Four from five is one. Now for the ace of spades."

He spells down and when he finishes naming the ace of spades, letter by letter, the magician holds but one card. He turns it face up. It is the ace of spades.

To perform this trick, simply arrange the four aces on top of the deck; then four twos; then four threes and so on. Note, however, the positions of four cards. The ace of spades should be the top ace of the aces. The five of clubs is the top of the fives; the nine of diamonds the top of the diamonds; the king of hearts on the very bottom of the pack.

The mere action of going through the deals as described, with their automatic card reversals, will make the trick work in the manner indicated.

7. AUTOMATIC SPELLING

The magician takes a number of cards from the pack. He gives the little packet to be shuffled. He asks a spectator to deal it into two heaps, one card at a time. The spectator is to look at the last card, remember it and lay it on either heap. The other heap is then dropped upon it.

We will suppose that the ace of hearts is the one selected. The magician takes the packet and asks for the name. It is given. He deals the top card of the packet face up, saying "A". The next card goes beneath the packet. Another is turned up, saying "C". Then one beneath. So on, spelling "E—O-F—H-E-A-R-T-S". When the magician announces the letter "S", he is holding a single card in his hand. He turns it up. It is the ace of hearts!

The secret depends upon the fact that when a group of eleven cards are spelled in this fashion, the sixth, or center card, will be the last one left. That is why the magician instructs the spectator to deal two heaps, look at the last card and lay it between the heaps, when they are gathered. It puts the chosen card right where he wants it.

All the cards in the packet must be spelled with exactly eleven letters. Here is a good line-up to use:

Ace of hearts, ace of spades, jack of clubs, six of spades, four of clubs, two of hearts, ten of spades, king of clubs, five of clubs, two of spades, ten of hearts.

There are just eleven cards in the group. Remember that those eleven are shuffled before one is selected. As a variation in the spelling, the magician may allow the person to spell mentally the name of his card, letter by letter, each time a card is dealt face up. The magician does not know the name of the card at all!

8. TWELVE CARD SPELLER The magician gives a cluster of cards to a spectator, tells him to shuffle the cards and to deal them into three heaps. Then the person is told to look at the bottom card of any heap and to place the heap between the other two.

Once again, the magician gathers the packet and spells, turning up a card for each letter and putting one under after each letter. In this case he also arrives at the selected card for the grand finish.

In this method, twelve cards are utilized instead of eleven.

They are all cards that may be spelled with twelve letters: for instance—five of hearts, queen of clubs, jack of spades, eight of clubs, seven of clubs, king of hearts, three of clubs, five of spades, jack of hearts, king of spades, four of spades, four of hearts.

With twelve cards, the eighth from the top will be the one left when the spelling deal is completed. By having the cards first dealt into three heaps, after the shuffle there are three groups of four cards each.

The process of looking at the bottom card of any heap and placing that heap between the other two heaps automatically makes the chosen card lie number eight from the top. It is the most natural type of procedure. Yet all the magician needs to do is go through his spelling bee and he finishes with the desired card in his possession.

This trick and the "Automatic Speller" can be worked into a very effective combination. Take any pack and get eleven eleven-letter cards together; beneath them twelve twelve-letter cards. Deal off the eleven and emphasize the shuffle and choice of card after dealing two heaps. Spell to that card. Repeat the trick, letting the spectator spell silently. Shuffle the group back into the pack, or place it on the bottom and deal off twelve cards. Then use the three-heap method.

Never state the exact number of cards that you are using in the trick. Take them off casually and let the audience think that you are using a number at random. Persons attempting to duplicate the stunt will invariably get a mixture of cards that spell with varied numbers of letters.

9. YANKEE DOODLE   A very clever variation of the spelling trick. A card is selected and returned to the pack which is handed to a spectator, with the request that he sing "Yankee

Doodle" and deal cards in rhythm with the song. So the person begins:

> *Yank*-ee *Doo*-dle *came* to *town*
> *Ri*-ding *on* a *po-ny*
> *Stuck* a *feath*-er *in* his *hat*
> And *called* it *mac-a-ro-ni*

The syllables in italics represent the beats on which cards are dealt and on the last card, the magician stops the dealer while he still has the card in his hand. Asking for the name of the card, the magician asks that the final card be turned up and it proves to be the one selected.

The dealing during this trick always ends on the sixteenth card as will be seen from the key syllables. Therefore, if the chosen card is planted at the sixteenth position, it will surely arrive at the finish.

To place the card, begin by running or sliding the cards of the face down pack from left hand to right, counting fifteen as you go. Keep the cards slightly separated at that point and continue shifting cards, asking someone to take a card from near the center of the pack.

After the card is drawn and noted, lift the top fifteen with the right hand and have the card replaced there. This puts the card at the right position. If desired, a few false shuffles or cuts may be made before the "Yankee Doodle" deal begins.

10. THE REPEAT SPELLER   This is really a trick that begins where all others leave off. Usually a "speller" ends when the magician has revealed a chosen card by that system. In the "Repeat Speller" he does the same trick time after time, always with the same result, a perfect spelling to the chosen card.

The effect is convincing from the start. Spreading the pack the magician allows a person to remove a card from any spot. Squaring the pack, he insists that the card be pushed fairly in the center. Asking the name of the card, the magician snaps the pack and begins to spell the card, dealing all cards face up, each falling upon the one before.

At the finish of the spelling, the magician turns up the chosen card. Then, gathering the cards, glancing through the pack and cutting it a few times, he repeats the trick with another person. There is always free choice of a card and it is invariably replaced in the center of the pack, yet the spelling never fails, for the simple reason that it can't. The whole working of the trick is practically automatic.

This form of the "speller" requires a special pack of cards, but it is the sort that can be easily assembled. It is made up from four identical packs of cards. Out of each pack you must take the following cards: Three, Seven, Eight, Queen of Hearts; Three, Seven, Eight, Queen of Spades; Ace, Two, Six, Ten of Diamonds; Joker.

Arrange the four groups in exactly the same order. That is, mix one so that its various suits will not be together; then arrange the remaining groups to match the first. Assemble these one upon the other. You will then be ready for the trick.

Every one of those cards can be spelled with exactly thirteen letters, as: Q-U-E-E-N—O-F—S-P-A-D-E-S. For the Joker, the spelling is: T-H-E—J-O-L-L-Y—J-O-K-E-R. Now, because there are four groups, every card in the pack is duplicated at the beginning of the next group. That is, in your pack of fifty-two, every thirteenth card is the same. The pack may be cut—in single cuts—as often as you wish, but this will not be changed as the groups form a rotation.

142

When the pack is spread and a card withdrawn by a spectator, the magician cuts the pack at that point, putting the top portion on the bottom, a very natural procedure. This puts a duplicate of the selected card at position thirteen. No one knows this, because the pack is kept face down. The end of the pack is riffled and the chosen card is replaced near the center, which is below that important thirteenth card.

All is then ready for the spelling. In this speller, the magician turns the cards face up as he deals them on the table, one upon another. This is a subtle way of showing that the cards are different. Of course only the top thirteen are different, but the spelling ends on the last card of that group and with it, the magician is showing the selected card.

By dealing each card face up on the one before, the magician has preserved the rotation. He gathers up that batch of cards, puts them face down on top of the pack. This fixes the set-up again, except that there is an odd card about the middle of the pack, the card that was actually selected and replaced there.

Turning the faces of the cards toward himself, the magician runs through the pack and finds this stray card, which is easy, because he knows what it is and about where it should be. He draws that card out and places it either on top or bottom of the pack. He gives the pack a few cuts, with the faces toward himself, merely as an excuse for the previous action, commenting that he will mix the cards.

Turning the pack face down, he has someone else select a card and with it he repeats the spelling trick precisely as before. This goes on as often as the magician wishes. Always, people are flabbergasted at seeing the selected card turn up and they never suspect any trickery in the slight maneuvers that follow.

All this is abetted by the fact that no one has any idea that duplicate cards are being used and the face-up deal diverts suspicion from that point. Though in the spelling the magician is always dealing the same cards face up, no one notices this because thirteen cards are too many to remember at sight and the rotation always begins at a different card.

Chapter 10

STRINGS AND ROPES

TRICKS WITH STRING AND ROPE HAVE BECOME A BRANCH of magic all their own, with enough variations to make a complete specialty of such work. Such tricks can be applied to every type of performance, from impromptu stunts to stage magic.

This chapter covers tricks that require other objects along with rope or string, thus giving the reader a wide range of ideas. There are so many good effects available that it is wiser to concentrate upon those which are simple and direct, rather than go into the intricate details of fancy knots which require too much study and practice.

Most string tricks can be worked with rope as well and in either case, the string or rope used should be smooth and easy to handle in order to facilitate the work. Soft rope is best for practically all tricks with rope.

All moves with string or rope should be practiced until they can be done both smoothly and rapidly as this impresses the observer and makes it much more difficult to detect any trickery involved.

1. AUTOMATIC KNOTS This is a showy bit of rope manipulation that appears to require a great deal of skill, but which can be learned after a few trials. Holding a length of rope across the outspread palms of his hands, the magician gives a few deft twists and immediately produces a knot in each end of the rope.

In substance, this means that the magician ties two one-hand knots simultaneously and since the action of the hands are identical, it will be explained on a one-hand basis. The palm is upward with the rope lying across it, with about eight inches

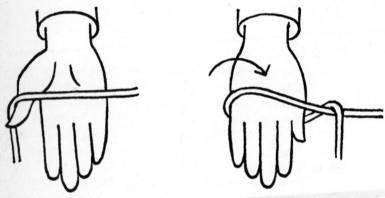

hanging over beyond the thumb. Holding the rope lightly, the hand is turned inward, forming a loop in the rope. The fingers are then pointed straight down, and are spread to keep the rope from falling away.

The loose end of the rope should now be hanging in front of the main portion. The dangling rope is clipped between the first two fingers. The fingers draw this rope straight upward through a self-forming loop and at the same time, the hand shakes the loose loop down and off.

With the thumb aiding, the end is drawn taut, the hand working over toward the very end of the rope, which runs itself free from the tightening knot. Done with two hands, the operation is simultaneous, each hand producing a knot and both drawing the ends of the rope.

2. THE DOUBLE LOOP   Slip a loop of string over a person's forefinger, follow it with a second loop—and *both* loops slide off the finger.

This trick is easy to do but must be performed rapidly. With your left hand, hold one end of the loop, dropping the other over the spectator's finger. Put your right forefinger against the middle of the two strings and, with your left hand, put the end of the loop over the person's forefinger.

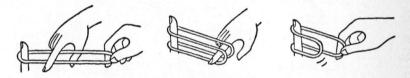

The loop is hooked twice over the spectator's finger, but when you release one of the strings with your right hand and hold the other as you draw your hand away, the result is a single loop.

3. SNAP A KNOT   Holding a short length of rope with both ends in his right hand, the magician gives one end of the rope a downward snap. Gathering up the end he repeats this a few times and on the final snap a double knot appears in the end of the rope.

The trick is easy but neat. Tie the knots in the end of the rope beforehand, but keep this end hidden in the hand while you give the other end a few snaps. On the last snap, just switch ends, letting the knotted end fly free. This gives the effect that the knots magically formed themselves.

4. LOOP TO LOOP In this trick the magician claims he will pass one solid object through another. He borrows a finger ring—takes a piece of string and ties a double knot, forming a loop beneath it. Then he places the ring on one end of the string and ties a double knot above it. The ring is captured in the upper loop and everyone agrees that it cannot be removed without untying the knots, both above and below it.

The performer then asks someone to hold the ends of the string, upon which he drapes a handkerchief over the upper knot, half way between the two ends. He reaches under the

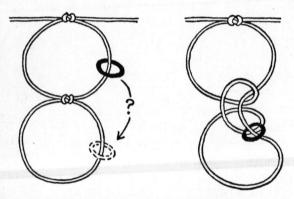

handkerchief and whisks the cloth away. The ring has passed from the upper loop to the lower—and the knots are still there!

The Method: The knot through which the ring must pass is a genuine knot—a double one. But the string actually goes through the knot, and since the ring is on the string, the ring can go through, too. Under the handkerchief, the magician loosens the double knot and slides the ring along the string, right through the knot and down to the lower loop. Then he tightens the double knot—takes the handkerchief away—and the trick is accomplished.

148

5. ON AND OFF MATCH-BOX   Using a tape or piece of string, the magician threads it through the cover of an empty match-box, letting some person hold the ends of the tape. The match-box is then covered with a handkerchief. Reaching beneath the cloth, the magician mysteriously removes the match-box from the tape, then lifts the handkerchief to show that the tape itself is quite intact.

This trick requires a definite type of match-box, namely one of the cardboard variety, the sort that usually contains blue-tip matches. Having acquired such a box, some special preparation becomes necessary. You will discover that in match-boxes of this type, the cover overlaps at one side; that is, it forms a double thickness, the two portions being glued together.

Carefully separate these connecting portions. Then prepare the separated surfaces with chewing gum, wax, or the gummy substance from a strip of Scotch tape. Do this sufficiently to make the two portions adhere as tightly as they were originally. Replace the drawer of the match-box in the cover and the trick is ready for presentation.

All that is necessary is to thread the tape through what appears to be a perfectly normal match-box. Under the handkerchief, separate the gummed portions of the cover and slide the match-box free of the tape. Press the sides of the cover back together again, making sure that they are good and tight; replace the drawer in the cover and bring out the match-box, intact. Like the tape, the match-box will stand sufficient examination to leave the witnesses completely baffled.

6. LOOP ON—LOOP OFF   A loop of string is placed over a spectator's forefinger, which should be held upright. The magician makes a few twists in the string, gathering it around his own thumb and fingers. He sets his forefinger upon the spectator's and the rope appears to be completely tangled.

Then, with a simple pull at the other end of the rope, the magician whips it free of the trapping fingers.

Use the right hand to make the twists, but all the while, the left should be drawing the other end of the rope fairly taut in order to facilitate the process which follows:

With the back of the right forefinger, lift the near string of the loop over the far string.

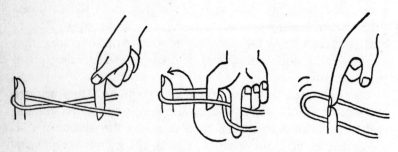

This forms a short loop close to the spectator's finger. Insert the right thumb into that short loop.

Now turn the right hand upward, with a rotary movement toward the left, so the right forefinger can be placed tip downward upon the top of the spectator's upraised finger.

Work the right thumb free from its loop and give the string a pull with the left hand.

That's all there is to this quick deceptive trick, but a few details should be emphasized. Have the knot at the end of the loop held by the left hand; in fact, the string does not have to be knotted if the left hand holds both ends.

Also, in twisting the hand, make sure that the string does not slip free. Right thumb and forefinger can press together to keep their respective loops in place.

7. BALL ON ROPE   Rolling a ball along a length of rope is a fine piece of jugglery, one which might take years to acquire—if ever.

Yet the trick is quite easy to do if you know the secret. First read the effect; then the explanation will make itself plain.

Taking a rope about two feet in length, the magician picks up a small ball and holds it in his right hand, which also grips one end of the rope. The rope is drawn taut between the hands and the right hand lets the ball roll onto the rope. As the left hand tilts downward, the ball runs toward it, only to change direction when the tilt is made the other way.

Finally the ball reaches one hand and is displayed there while the other hand tosses the rope away.

The ball used should be a light one, such as a hollow rubber or celluloid ball, though a wooden ball will do. The real trick, however is in the rope—or rather, what goes with it.

What goes with the rope is a white thread, slightly longer than the rope. This thread is wound around the rope at both ends; when the rope is dangled, the thread seems to be part of it.

When ready for the trick, the magician holds his hands upward and slips his thumbs between the rope and the thread, the latter being at the back. The ball is ready in the right fingers, when released toward the rope, it finds a track awaiting it, the track consisting of the rope and the hidden thread behind it. The ball runs right along the groove, according to the tilt.

8. THE IMPOSSIBLE KNOT   Taking a piece of string about twelve inches long, the magician ties it around the cover of a wooden match-box, forming a knot on the outside of the cover.

He puts the end of the string through the cover, then slides the knot from around the cover and pushes it inside, letting some person hold the ends of the string.

Everyone now knows that the knot is inside the match-box cover, because they saw it placed there. But when the person pulls the ends of the string and the magician runs the cover back and forth along it, the knot for some mysterious reason has completely disappeared and both string and match-box cover may be examined.

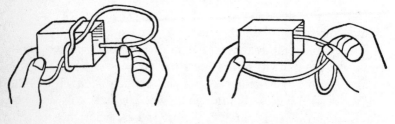

This is called the "Impossible Knot" because that is exactly what it is. If the trick is properly performed the knot disposes of itself. Just follow the instructions carefully and you will not only see for yourself but will then be in a position to mystify your friends, and thoroughly.

First tie the knot, a simple single knot, around the match-box cover, so that one end of the string leads off to the right, over the end of the cover. Hold the cover upright and drop that end of the string down through the cover. Let a person hold that end of the string with one hand. Then draw the whole knot off the right end of the cover; bundle the knot inside. Let the person hold the other end of the string in his other hand.

The trick is done by that time. Actually, you have put the end of the string *back through* the knot, or single loop, thus untying it. When the spectator pulls the ends of the string, just run the match-box cover back and forth and show that the knot has vanished!

9. ROPE AND VASE MYSTERY   The magician shows a rounded vase and a two-foot length of thin rope. He inserts the end of the rope in the vase and winds the rest of the rope about the neck.

Inverting the vase, the magician lets the rope dangle downward. Oddly, it does not drop from the vase, but hangs sus-

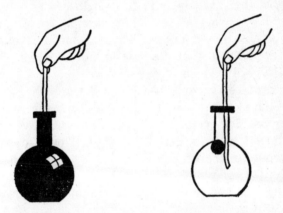

pended there. Lifting the hanging end of the rope, the magician lowers the vase. This time, the mystery is reversed. The vase hangs, unsupported, from the rope.

The magician commands the vase to swing back and forth. It does so. He orders it to stop; it stands still. Next, at his command, the vase begins to swing in a large circle. Finally, he grasps the vase and removes the rope.

Both items may then be examined by the spectators, with no clue to the mystery.

Inside the vase is a little rubber ball. Its diameter, plus

153

that of the rope, must be a little greater than the width of the neck of the vase.

In winding the rope about the neck of the vase, tilt the vase mouth downward. The ball will slide into the neck. A slight tightening of the rope will grip the ball in place.

The rope will then hang when the vase is inverted. Conversely, the vase will cling to the rope. The final effect, the swinging of the vase, is accomplished by an unnoticeable motion of the hand that holds the rope.

Simply let the vase dangle at full length of the rope. When you want it to swing in pendulum fashion, your hand will respond, although you do not have to move it purposely. Similarly, when you want the vase to stop, you will find that your muscles will tighten.

You can make it swing in a circle through the same subconscious impulse. To conclude the trick, grip the vase by the neck with your left hand. Hold the neck between your thumb and forefinger, with the left hand cupped palm upward below the mouth of the vase.

Pull out the rope with the right hand. A steady draw will remove the rope and the ball will drop unnoticed into the left hand.

The ball is in the vase at the start, unless you prefer to allow a preliminary examination of the vase and rope. In that case, you must have the ball between the thumb and fingers of your hand. In receiving the vase, take it at the mouth and let the ball drop into the vase.

10. THE STRUNG CARDS In this trick the magician uses a dozen playing cards, which he prepares by punching holes near the ends. Ribbons run through each end, so that the cards form the rungs of a miniature ladder.

The cards are drawn back and forth along the ribbons. Each ribbon is pulled separately in one direction, then in the other. The magician states that he will use either ribbon in the trick, so he asks the spectators to choose one.

With one ribbon selected, the magician winds the other about the ends of the cards and ties it in place. He holds the loose ribbon upward and draws it back and forth. Spreading

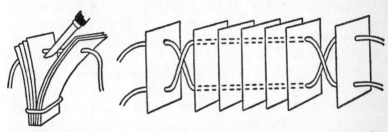

the loose ends of the cards, he shows the ribbon between the cards and asks the spectators to cut it with a pair of scissors.

That done, the magician announces that the cut ribbon will manifest a curious restoration. After a few moments, he pulls one end of the loose ribbon. It runs through the cards just as it did before. The cut ribbon is restored.

To conclude this demonstration, the magician lets a person take the short end of the restored ribbon. The magician walks away with the cards; the ribbon comes completely clear. It is then in the hands of the spectators who can examine it and see that the restoration is complete.

Nine cards are used and they conceal a peculiar arrangement of the ribbons. To prepare the trick, thread the ribbons through the cards. Hold the cards flat and turn the top card end around. Turn the pack over and do the same with the card that was originally the bottom one of the stack.

The ribbons are thus criss-crossed beneath each end card.

155

This cannot be seen, since the cards are held in a stack. When you pull one ribbon back and forth, it appears to run straight through the cards. The same is the case with the other ribbon.

It makes no difference which ribbon is chosen. Simply wind the other around its end of the cards to keep it in place, but do not tie it too tightly, as you want a little play between the cards.

Hold the loose end of the cards upward, pull the chosen ribbon back and forth a few times more and finally center it. Then spread the cards near the middle, and invite someone to cut the ribbon.

The spectator thinks he is cutting the loose ribbon. Actually, he is cutting the center of the lower ribbon. After the cut, you have merely to draw the loose ribbon back and forth. It will run as freely as before.

When someone takes the end of the loose ribbon, you can walk away and the ribbon will run free from the cards. That leaves the restored ribbon in the hands of the spectators.

11. THE TRAPPED TRAPPER   The magician takes a piece of string and ties the ends to form a large loop about two feet in length. Crossing his hands, he draws two lengths of string to form an "X" inside the large loop. This produces two inner loops.

He then asks someone to insert a finger in the loop at the left. That done, the magician pulls the right end of the string. The loops tighten and trap the spectator's finger.

Forming the loops again, the magician inserts his own finger, using his left hand. He pulls the string from the right and the loops slide away, leaving his left finger free. They seem to pass right through the finger.

Every time the trick is repeated, the result is the same. The loops are formed in the same fashion, but the spectator's finger is always trapped; the magician's invariably comes free.

There are two ways of forming the loops so nearly alike that they appear to be identical. One system will trap the finger—the other will not.

Make a large loop and hold it taut between the hands, one end of the loop girdling your left fingers, the other the right. Hold your palms upward.

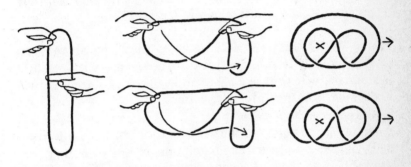

Swing the right hand over to the left. With your right thumb and forefinger grasp the string just *below* the little finger of the left hand. Draw the right hand away, carrying the string with it.

Bring the left hand over to the right and use the left thumb and forefinger to grasp the string just *below* the little finger of the right hand. In doing this, bring the left thumb and forefinger *above* the string grasped between the right thumb and forefinger.

Stretch the string between your hands. The loops are formed. Lay them carefully upon the table, keeping the hands palm upward as you do so. The loops are ready for the release. If you place your forefinger in the little loop at the left and

157

draw away the outer string at the right, the loops will come clear.

The other method of forming the loops differs in one detail. When you bring your left hand over to the right to grasp the string below the right little finger, reach *beneath* the string that is held by the right thumb and forefinger, instead of *above* it.

Formed by this system, the loops will look exactly the same when laid upon the table—but this time, they will trap any finger that is placed in the loop at the left.

12. STRING THE RINGS Finger rings, metal washers, Chinese coins—even large disks of wood, with holes bored in the centers, will work equally well in this trick. String is used if the rings are small; for larger ones, like curtain rings, rope is preferable.

One ring is knotted to the center of the cord. Next the two ends of the cord are raised and the rest of the rings are dropped on so they fall upon the knotted ring. The two ends of the cord are separated; each is given to a spectator.

Reaching beneath the cloth, the magician removes all the rings and brings them out. The handkerchief is lifted to prove that they are the same rings. Everything may then be examined.

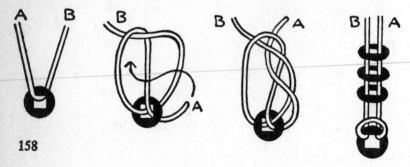

It all lies in the tying of the first ring. Run the cord through the ring and tie a single knot, forming a large loop. The left side of the loop should be at the front of the ring. The right end of the string should be at the front of the knot. Now run that end through the ring from the front, bring it around, up and through the knot from the front.

This gives the effect of a triple knot, but actually the ring has been placed in a position for release. Leave the knots slightly loose so they will look like knots while the other rings are threaded on the double cord. When the handkerchief covers the rings, reach beneath and pull the knot tight. It becomes a loop which can be spread down over the sides of the ring and drawn free, releasing the bottom ring and all those above it.

Chapter 11

DIFFERENT TRICKS

THE TRICKS IN THIS CHAPTER HAVE BEEN SELECTED largely because of their practicability in performance, with particular emphasis upon those that will stand the test of close-up performance. They come under the head of general magic, because they require a variety of objects, but nothing elaborate is needed to perform them.

In fact, most of these tricks come within the range of Pocket Magic, so far as portability is concerned. With some, borrowed articles may be used and it is easy enough to carry whatever else may be needed.

None of these tricks is very difficult; few require much practice, so far as the actual acquiring of the method is concerned. But they all need proper presentation and therefore they should be rehearsed with care. In order to impress people, tricks must be done smoothly and convincingly; also, where some special maneuver is required, any clumsy or belated movement can prove fatal at that crucial time.

The reader will recognize this as he tries out certain of the tricks; therefore he should make plenty of those trials privately before attempting such tricks in public.

1. TORN AND RESTORED PAPER   The magician shows a strip of thin paper, and tears it into pieces. He has shown his hands absolutely empty; and when he folds up the torn pieces, he keeps them constantly in sight.

But when the papers are unfolded, they are restored into a single strip!

The trick must be performed with a special crepe paper, which may be purchased in narrow rolls at stationery stores. This paper can be stretched to twice its length.

The magician begins with a single sheet of paper, about twelve inches long and only about an inch in width. He tears it deliberately in half; then he tears it some more; but he only tears one section of the paper. The result is that he has a six inch strip remaining when he folds the torn pieces.

He holds this in his left hand, calling attention to the fact that the end of the paper is always in view. With his right hand he draws the paper slowly between his left thumb and forefinger, exerting pressure so that the paper stretches as it emerges.

The result is that he draws forth a twelve inch strip of paper —presumably the piece with which he began—but in reality, half of the original strip!

The "getaway" or disposal of the torn pieces is an important item. Inasmuch as only one strip is used, there is little suspicion of remaining pieces. If the performer is near a table or a chair, he can easily drop them (folded tightly) on the floor.

In the open, the best plan is to show the right hand empty, and to moisten the fingers every now and then while drawing out the restored strip. While doing this, the right thumb and fingers take hold of the extra pieces and leave them in the mouth during the second or third moistening process. The tongue pushes the paper up in the cheek.

161

Another plan is to tear off a corner of the original strip, and to keep that corner in view all the time. After the paper is folded, it is transferred from the right hand to the left; but the extra pieces are kept in the right.

As the left hand shows the complete piece folded up with the corner still in view, the right hand has plenty of opportunity to pocket the extra pieces without suspicion.

A clever plan is to use a ruler to show the approximate length of the paper. Put the ruler in the pocket. Show the hands empty and proceed. As the paper is drawn out in one hand, the other reaches in the pocket for the ruler, leaving the extra pieces there.

Both measurements should be made quickly, as it is likely that the paper will vary slightly before and after the restoration.

2. PENCIL FROM MATCH-BOX   A very surprising trick. The magician takes a match-box from his pocket, opens it and extracts a full-length pencil.

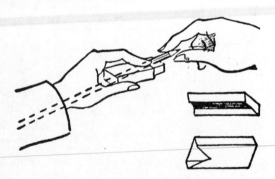

The box must be prepared beforehand. It is an ordinary safety-match box; but the inner end of the drawer is cut away, and a V-shaped space is made in the bottom of the cover, running from the end toward the center.

The pencil is up the left sleeve.

The right hand places the box in the left, and moving toward the wrist, grasps the end of the pencil and draws it forward. The drawer of the box is opened, and the right hand slides the box back into the left hand so that the end of the pencil comes inside. Then reaching into the box, he draws the pencil directly through.

3. KNIFE THROUGH THE HANDKERCHIEF This is another trick with an improvement; both methods will be described under one heading.

The magician borrows a pen-knife and a handkerchief. The handkerchief is spread out and the corners are held by spectators. A square sheet of paper, smaller than the handkerchief, is placed upon the cloth. Then the magician lowers the knife under the handkerchief, and states that he will try to cut the paper without injuring the handkerchief—something that appears impossible.

He taps the handkerchief several times, causing the paper to bob up and down. Suddenly he pulls the knife right through the paper—yet the handkerchief is uninjured!

This is all done during the preliminary part of the trick. As he taps the paper through the handkerchief, the magician holds the knife in his right hand. As if by accident, he knocks the paper to the edge of the handkerchief. There the left hand takes the side of the paper, thumb above and fingers beneath. The right hand has moved over also and the left fingers grip the handle of the knife.

The left hand lifts the paper and drops it back on the center of the handkerchief; and it lets the knife fall between the handkerchief and the sheet of paper. Meanwhile the right hand keeps tapping the bottom of the handkerchief as though it still held the knife. Then it grips the knife through the cloth, tilts the blade upward, and pushes it through the paper, the left hand helping.

The paper is pierced with the knife—yet the handkerchief is uninjured.

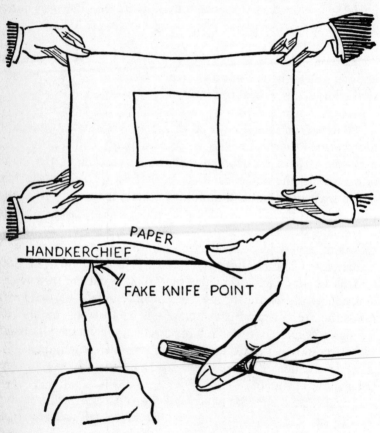

PAPER

HANDKERCHIEF

FAKE KNIFE POINT

In the improvement, the magician has the end of a knife blade or a pointed bit of metal hidden in his right hand. He places the paper on the handkerchief; then withdraws it and deliberately exchanges the knife from hand to hand under the paper. But he instantly puts the right hand under the center of the handkerchief and pushes the point of the hidden blade against the center of the cloth.

He lets people feel the point of the knife through the cloth. Then he drops the paper upon it, and the actual knife goes along with the paper.

The concealment of the dull knife blade in the right hand is not at all difficult. Some magicians have it attached to an elastic that runs up the sleeve, but this is really unnecessary.

4. THROUGH THE COAT This is an effective variation of the previous trick. The magician removes his coat and lays it over the back of an open-backed chair, the back of the coat being toward the audience.

His right hand holds a knife and lowers it behind the coat, while the left hand holds a sheet of paper in front of the coat.

Suddenly the sheet of paper is pierced by the knife, which makes its appearance through the uninjured coat.

The magician simply drops the knife in the collar of the coat as he lowers his right hand. While the right forefinger taps against the center of the coat to indicate the presence of the knife, the left hand raises the paper to show the center of the coat. The left thumb and forefinger are behind the sheet of paper and they pick up the knife, carrying it under the paper to the center of the coat in front. Then the right hand grips the knife through the coat and the left hand pulls the knife through the paper.

With an extra knife blade, the right hand can show the

actual point of the knife at the center of the coat, when the left hand lifts the paper. The extra blade may be easily dropped in the inside coat pocket.

5. SELF RISING MATCH-BOX   A match-box is laid *across* the fingers of the left hand. Suddenly it rises, very slowly; then it sinks again. It is finally handed for examination.

The Method: Open the box very slightly in an inward direction. Set that end of the box upon the third finger of the left hand. Close the box with the right hand, catching a very tiny bit of flesh on the left finger.

Now the slightest tipping of the hand will control the box. Even the natural shaking of the fingers is sufficient. With a little practice the performer can make the box rise and fall at will, with no unnatural motion of the left hand.

The right hand in taking the box opens it slightly so it can be removed from the left fingers. People may watch as closely as they desire, yet the magician makes the box obey every command without hesitation.

166

6. WHISK-AWAY COIN   A borrowed handkerchief is laid on the table. A coin is placed in the center. The handkerchief is folded, the ends are pulled—the coin is gone. The handkerchief is returned to its owner.

You must experiment with this trick in order to learn the exact procedure. Once you have practiced it, you will find it most simple of execution.

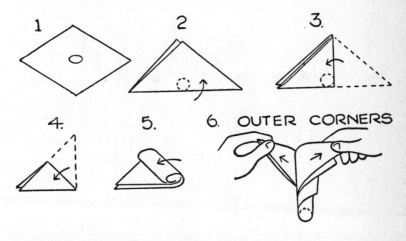

The coin is laid in the center of the cloth, which is folded diagonally to form a triangle. Fold this triangle in half, then in half again.

Roll the cloth, beginning with the side where the coin is located. Then comes the important move.

You will note two corners of the handkerchief, one within the other. Draw these corners rather smartly, one with each hand. The handkerchief will come out straight. The coin is hidden in its center crease.

To all appearances, the coin has vanished. You are holding

167

the cloth horizontally. To return the handkerchief, carefully raise one end so that the cloth approaches the vertical.

Sliding down the crease, the coin will reach your lower hand and drop there unseen. The other hand shakes the handkerchief and returns it.

7. TWICE AROUND The magician wraps the handkerchief about a stick. He asks a person to place his finger upon the

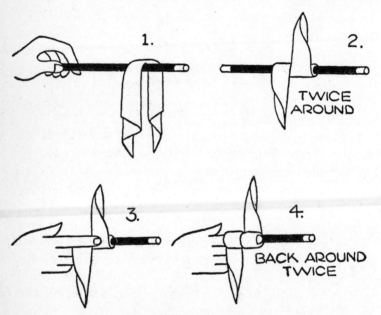

upper side of the handkerchief while he (the magician) continues the wrapping. A few more twists, the ends of the handkerchief are tied and the finger removed. Both ends of the stick are held. With a quick yank the magician pulls the handkerchief free of the stick.

Lay the handkerchief over the center of the stick so the ends dangle. Carry the ends under the stick and over. Let the ends drop. Again carry the ends under the stick and over. While you still hold the ends ask the person to place his finger on the handkerchief above the stick.

When you continue to wrap the handkerchief about the stick carry each end *back in the direction from which it came* so the ends go over both finger and stick. Let the ends drop. Carry the ends under the finger and stick, bring them up and tie them over the finger. Ask the person to remove his finger from the handkerchief.

Although you have apparently wrapped the handkerchief about the stick your real action has been to first wrap and then unwrap it, thanks to the spectator's finger. While both ends of the stick are held, simply pull the handkerchief at the knot and the handkerchief will come free.

The one point to remember while doing the trick is not to cross the ends while you are carrying them about the stick. Simply follow the procedure as given and practice until it can be done without hesitation.

8. OFF WITH HIS HEAD   The magician states that he will demonstrate a novel means of execution used in China, chopping off a head with a rope. He uses a wooden match to represent the Chinaman. Lighting the match, the magician burns the head, then blows out the flame. He holds the match with the head upward.

From his own head, the magician takes a hair and winds it about the neck of the miniature Chinaman. He gives the hair a sharp tug. Instantly, the head pops from the match.

The match is burned with the head held upward so that only a short stretch of burned wood supports the match head. The match is held between the thumb and forefinger of the right hand in an upright position.

Allow about a quarter inch of the match to project below the right forefinger. Have the second finger pressed against that lower tip. The left hand then pretends to take a hair and wind it around the bottom of the match head.

The left hand makes a quick tug to the left, as though pulling the imaginary hair. As you jerk the left hand, snap your right second finger inward. The leverage against the lower end of the match will cause the match head to pop off. The sudden motion of the left hand draws attention from the quick snap of the right second finger.

9. SAFETY PIN SNAPPER Two safety pins are locked together. The magician takes the safety pins and clicks them one way, then another, to show that they are firmly fastened. Suddenly, he draws the safety pins apart and hands them immediately to the spectators. The pins are separated, yet each one is clamped as firmly as before.

The trick is simply to pull the safety pins so that the bar of one slides between the point and clasp of the other so neatly that the second pin snaps back to closed position. To do this, you must know the exact way in which to hold the pins.

Close one safety pin. Hold it by the small end. Keep it level, with the clasp away from you and the loose bar to the *right*. Push the point of the other pin straight up, just to the *left* of the loose bar of the first pin. Clasp the second pin.

Swing the second pin so its solid bar is toward you, and lay it downward to the left, so it is almost flat upon the first pin. The clasp of the second pin is toward your left. Take the clasp of the second pin between your right thumb and forefinger, the thumb above.

While the left thumb and forefinger firmly hold the small end of the first pin, slide your right hand forward and to the right. It pulls the second pin by the clasp. The solid bar of the second pin comes under the clasp of the first pin and the second pin slides free. The first pin will clasp again.

10. THE ADROIT DOLLAR BILL This is the mystery of the dollar bill that turns itself upside down at the magician's

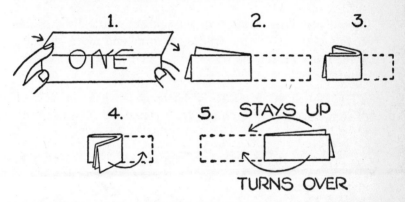

command. Holding the bill upright between his hands, the front of the bill toward the spectators, the magician folds it and then unfolds it again. The bill is right side up when he starts; naturally it is the same when he finishes. But that is only the first process. When the magician repeats the folding and unfolding, the bill has turned itself upside down.

Hold the bill as described. Fold the top half forward and down, making a long strip. Fold the right half frontwise to the left, making a shorter strip. Fold the right half frontwise to the left again.

Now unfold the back half of the bill, which consists of two doubled corners, swinging them to the right. Swing the front half of the bill to the left. Bring the front portion of the bill upward and you are right where you started, everything fair and normal.

To make the bill turn topsy-turvy, you change just one move. Fold it exactly as you did before. In unfolding, swing those two back corners over to the right. Then comes the different move: Swing the back half of the bill to the left. Now lift the front portion of the bill and it will be showing upside down.

Practice these moves until they work automatically and the acrobatics of the dollar bill will prove more and more puzzling every time you repeat the trick.

11. THE PASSING KNOTS   The magician has two sets of handkerchiefs, three in each set. Red, white and blue were the

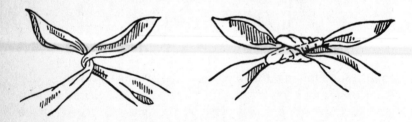

original colors. Then all whites came into common use. The best combination is to have two reds and a blue in one set, two blues and a red in the other.

The magician picks up the two blues and a red; and places them in a tumbler or on a stand. Then he ties the blue between the two reds. Shaking these three handkerchiefs, the blue handkerchief falls free. Upon lifting the other set of silks, the red is seen to be tied between the two blues!

There are two phases to the trick: first, the vanishing of the knots from the first set; second, the appearance of the knots in the second set.

The first is accomplished by tying a trick knot. If an ordinary square knot is tied with the corners of two handkerchiefs, it will become a slip-knot if one corner is tied around the other. Tie the red around the blue, then pull the blue handkerchief straight, and it can be drawn free from the red.

But the quick vanishing knot is tied thus: simply cross the corners of the blue and the red like a letter X. Bend the red under the blue and the blue over the red. Hold each handkerchief with the third and fourth fingers of the hands, while the thumbs and first two fingers tie a single knot with the corners.

This knot can be drawn very tightly. It will not pass the twist originally formed. Yet a mere shake of the handkerchiefs will cause the separation. In making the twist, the hands should be kept in motion, imitating the tying of a single knot.

The appearance of the knots in the other group of silks is simple: the knots are already there, but the side tips of the silks are tied, and not the upper and lower corners. The knots are concealed in the folds of the silks. The handkerchiefs are rolled together; when they are unrolled, grasp the side corner of one of the blue handkerchiefs, and shake them into a string of three.

12. THE AMAZING BEAD TRICK This is a modernized version of the old Hindu Needle Trick, wherein the magician pretends to swallow some needles and thread; then draws the needles from his mouth, all threaded. Not only was the Needle Trick dangerous, it belonged strictly among freak acts and was originally used only by side-show performers. Performed with beads, the trick is safe and can be presented rather tastefully.

The magician shows a long string of beads and holds it above a small glass. Taking a pair of scissors, he cuts the string and the beads fall into the glass. Pouring the beads into his hand, the wizard places them in his mouth, then rolls up some cotton thread and places it in his mouth too.

Finding the end of the thread, the magician slowly draws it into sight and the beads come along, being magically threaded and allowing the whole string to be shown completely strung together.

The deception is very neat. Actually, the beads are strung together all the time, though the audience does not suspect it. In arranging the beads, first string them to a thread, knotting beads at each end, and leaving it reasonably loose.

Next thread the beads again, this time using a colored string and adding a few loose beads on each end. The string should have a large, conspicuous knot at the bottom.

In cutting the cord, insert the scissors just above the bottom bead. This will be below the lowermost bead of the group that is also threaded. Cut the string and the beads will fall into the glass just as if they were really loose. In landing, they will coil because the thread is slack and everyone will now believe that the beads are really separate.

Adding to that illusion are the odd beads from the ends of the cord, which may bounce from the glass and can in any event be shown as stray beads later. This happens when the magician pours the beads from the glass into his hand, where again they will seem separated and the few free beads will spill to the table, where the magician ignores them, since his hand contains enough for a sizeable mouthful.

The beads are placed in the mouth; then a piece of thread is gathered and added to them. This thread is simply thrust up to the side of the cheek by the tongue. Meanwhile, the magician finds an end bead with his fingers and slowly draws out the whole line, all mysteriously threaded.

If any of the extra beads are put into the mouth, they can be pressed up beside the upper gum along with the thread. It is just as well however to let them remain on the table or gather them and drop them back into the glass, as there is then no hazard from having unthreaded beads in the mouth and the stray beads definitely convince observers that the whole string must have been broken.

In this form, the trick is definitely self-working and proves a very effective mystery.

13. RICE AND CHOPSTICK A bottle is filled with rice. The magician takes a chopstick and presses it down through the neck of the bottle, deep into the rice. He says a few Chinese words and lifts the end of the chopstick. The bottle-load of rice comes up from the table.

Simply press the chopstick firmly. The rice will do the rest. The pressure of the stick forces rice to the sides of the bottle. Wedged in a mass, the grains choke the bottle neck and the rice grips the chopstick with the right. The stick will come out easily.

A transparent bottle is preferable, as the rice can then be seen inside it. A rounded bottle, or any of an unusual shape naturally looks better than an ordinary medicine bottle, therefore an odd bottle should be used, if obtainable.

14. COLOR-CHANGING BALLOON Showing a blue balloon, the magician calls particular attention to its color and exhibits the balloon on all sides. Then, passing his hand over the balloon, he produces a most remarkable result. People hear the balloon suddenly explode, yet it still remains inflated. However, instead of being blue, the balloon has changed color and is now red.

Though more of a surprise than a trick, this will still be a perplexity if neatly presented as an incidental effect. Two balloons are used, a red and a blue. Beforehand, the red balloon is inserted inside the blue and the two are inflated together. The neck of the inner red is then tightened with a rubber band and more air is blown into the blue by stretching its neck to one side.

This forms an air-pocket between the inner red balloon and the outer blue. There is no need to tie the neck of the blue balloon as pressure from the red will keep it tight. When shown to the audience, it appears to be an ordinary blue balloon.

Holding the double neck away from the audience, the magician brings his other hand over the surface of the balloon. Between his fingers, he conceals a small pin. He touches this to the top of the blue balloon which promptly bursts, showing the red instead. The remnants of the blue rubber gather unnoticed at the neck of the red balloon which is out of sight and the pin is dropped on the floor.

15. BALANCED MATCH-BOXES   Here is a balancing feat that passes as a display of unusual skill, yet can be learned at first try, because there is a trick to it. Picking up some matchboxes, the performer sets one on top of another until he has a half a dozen or more all forming a precarious stack which does not fall even when he circles his hand quite rapidly.

It's done by neatly locking the boxes in place as you stack

them. In setting one box on top of the first, push the drawer of the upper box downward. It forces the drawer of the lower box into the hand, where the projecting end will not be seen.

Repeat this locking with each additional box and the whole stack will be quite firm. Keep the boxes high, so the top box, with its depressed drawer, is above the line of the audience's vision. By then, everyone will be convinced that as a balancer you are very adroit.

For a finish, strike the boxes with the free hand, scattering them all over the floor. This will knock some of them partly open, apparently proving that there is no fakery connected with the match-boxes. The real purpose of course is to cover up the subtle device that you used in balancing the boxes.

16. THE UPRIGHT HANDKERCHIEF The magician shows a freshly-ironed handkerchief and spreads it on the table. Taking the center, he lifts it. The handkerchief stands upright on the table.

Removing the handkerchief, the magician shows that there is nothing beneath it. He spreads the handkerchief upon his left hand; lifts the center with his right. This time, the handkerchief balances upon the hand.

The first part of the trick is designed to divert suspicion from the second stage. Similarly, the second balance offsets any doubt concerning the first.

The original balance is a simple matter. Merely draw up the center of the spread-out handkerchief and it will stand like a miniature pyramid, the pleats aiding in its support. After the balance, lift the handkerchief and call attention to the fact that there was nothing beneath it.

Do this wtih your right hand. In your left, you have a cylindrical ruler of the slide-out type. It is out of sight, for the back of your hand is toward the spectators. Drape the handkerchief over the left hand. Turn the left hand palm upward. Through the cloth, grip the end of the metal tape and draw it upward.

Simply steady the cylinder with thumb and fingers. It will stay in position while the stiff tape balances the handkerchief. Finally, push the center of the handkerchief downward with the right hand. Pocket the handkerchief with your left and let the metal cylinder drop in your pocket.

17. VANISHING PENCIL　This is an excellent surprise for any occasion where a pencil has been used, particularly after some other trick. Tearing a piece of newspaper, the magician rolls the pencil inside it and promptly tears the paper to shreds, showing that even pencils have ways of making themselves disappear.

A special pencil is used but it is easily prepared. Roll a piece of glazed paper around a pencil; glue the paper and slide it free. Into the tube thus formed, jam the stub of a pencil, letting the point project.

This can be handled like an ordinary pencil up to the time of the vanish. Then it is simply a case of rolling the "pencil" inside a sheet of paper, which can be promptly torn. Drop the paper pieces in your pocket; along with them goes the slightly longer section that contains the stub.

As an aftermath you can reach in your pocket and bring out a pencil of the same color, as if it were the one that vanished. The "Pencil From Match-box" (described in this chapter) is a good trick to use in order to bring back the vanished pencil.

18. THE CHANGING MATCH PACK　A surprising bit of magic, with the commonest objects, a pack of paper matches.

Showing such a pack, first on one side, then the other, the magician passes his hand over it, with an immediate result.

Instantly, the match pack changes both its color and its appearance. From red it becomes blue, with a new design printed on it. Again the magician introduces his magic pass and the pack is transformed back to its original state.

The match pack is not so innocent as it would seem. Actually it is a double pack: two instead of one. The device is very

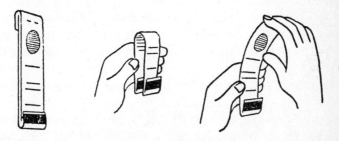

easily prepared from two ordinary match packs of different design. Open two such packs to their full length, remove the matches and place one pack upon the other, both with their printed sides outward, and with each pack inverted in relation to the other.

It is then quite simple to push the flap of one pack under the base of the other and vice versa. That is, the opened packs become interlocked. When these two packs are folded as if they were one, the printing of one pack comes to the outside; that of the other is hidden within.

Held in closed fashion, the double job appears to be an ordinary pack of matches which can be shown freely on both sides. When the other hand is passed over the pack, the hand that holds it releases pressure. The pack then flips open and the passing hand draws the upper half of the pack over and down, causing the inside to appear. The hand that holds the pack immediately grips it in its new position and the transformed pack may be shown as freely as before.

The change may be made by letting the front half of the pack flap backward when the hand passes over it. This is purely a matter of choice with the individual performer.

To handle the tricky pack most effectively, it should be well prepared beforehand. The two portions can be stapled or glued together so that they will operate neatly. Since this is a swift trick, it is important to have a striking contrast between the packs used to form the special pack. Then observers will be able to recognize the transformation the moment it occurs.

By having an ordinary pack to match one of the designs, the performer can make a switch at the conclusion of the trick. He should begin by saying that he wants a match; reaching in his pocket he brings out the faked pack. Changing it back and forth a few times, he replaces it in his pocket. Never having seen the inside of the pack, the spectators do not know that it is empty of matches.

Hence when the magician brings out the pack again, opens it and strikes a match, recalling that he wanted a light, there is no cause for suspicion. The pack that the magician brings out is the duplicate, a very ordinary pack that will stand inspection should anyone pick it up later.

Chapter 12

MENTAL MYSTERIES

ALTHOUGH MENTAL MYSTERIES ARE A VERY OLD FORM of magic, they have become so popular in recent years that many long-known effects are regarded as new. This simply proves that the worth of a trick does not depend upon how new it is, but how good it is.

There is also a psychological factor where mental tricks are concerned. People have become accustomed to skillful displays of sleight-of-hand. They know that objects do not actually appear from space and vanish into nowhere, even though they appear to do just that.

But when the effect is purely mental, witnesses are sometimes willing to believe that the impossible has happened. Thus mind reading tricks, either long-neglected or seldom seen, become a carry-over from the time when people were inclined to be credulous regarding feats of magic.

The performer should remember this when working even the simplest of mental effects. He will then find that he can build from one trick to another, with constantly increasing results. Also there are certain audiences that will prefer mental magic to other forms. It is good policy to be ready for them and the tricks in this chapter will provide the wherewithal.

1. CHOOSE YOUR WORD This mental mystery can be built to a very startling climax, as the magician seemingly names any word chosen from a dictionary, purely through the power of concentration.

Giving a small dictionary to a spectator, the magician asks him to name a number between one and four hundred, to signify a page; also another number between one and fifty, to represent a word on that page.

Supposing the spectator takes 162 and 38. He is told to open the dictionary to page 162, then count down 38 words and remember the word he finds there. The magician meanwhile steps out of the room, so he will have no opportunity to watch the spectator write the random word upon a slip of paper.

Returning, the magician picks up the slip of paper bearing the word and after due concentration names the very word that was selected.

Now for the artful secret. The dictionary used is of the small pocket type. The magician has _two_ copies of the dictionary but keeps one pocketed and does not show it. Knowing the number of the page and the word, the magician has only to consult the duplicate dictionary when he is out of the room. He does this while the spectator is looking up the word in the original dictionary.

The business of having the spectator write the word on a slip of paper upon which the performer later concentrates, is simply to draw attention from the real secret.

2. THE CALENDAR MYSTERY Using a sheet torn from an ordinary calendar, the performer introduces a puzzling mental mystery. Preferably, a month should be taken that has thirty-one days with dates running into five weeks—not six, as occasionally occurs.

By way of example, the following month is shown:

Sun	Mon	Tue	Wed	Thur	Fri	Sat
			1	2	3	4
5	6	7	8	9	10	11
12	13	14	15	16	17	18
19	20	21	22	23	24	25
26	27	28	29	30	31	

Handing the sheet to a spectator, the mental wizard asks him to pick one day in every week and mark it with a circle. This is done while the performer's back is turned. Thus, one date is chosen from the first week; another from the second; and so on.

Again in illustration, we will assume that the dates picked are: 3 - 7 - 13 - 19 - 31.

Now the performer asks the spectator to tell him how many Sundays were marked, but not which Sundays were specifically picked. He also asks for the number of Mondays, Tuesdays and so on. At no time, however, is the spectator asked to name any specific date or even any specific week.

That done, the magician names a large total. In this case he announces: "Seventy-three." He tells the person to add the total of the dates that he has marked and they come to that exact number.

Now for the method of the mystery. The performer begins by finding a key-number for himself, which makes the trick quite easy, since he memorizes the number and uses it as his basis. That number is found by adding up the Sundays, in this case 5, 12, 19 and 26, making a total of 62. Then the performer must deduct from the first week, if it begins later than a Sunday. For example, in the month shown, the first week actually reads;

$$-2 \quad -1 \quad 0 \quad 1 \quad 2 \quad 3 \quad 4$$

Therefore 2 is deducted from the total of 62, giving 60 as the key-number which the performer remembers.

When the performer asks how many Sundays have been marked, the answer does not matter, as the Sundays total to the key-number. But for every Monday marked, he mentally adds one; for every Tuesday two; Wednesday, three; Thursday, four; Friday, five; Saturday, six.

In the sample calendar, we assume that the spectator has marked one Monday (17) one Tuesday (7) and two Fridays (3 and 31). Hence the performer adds one, two, and ten respectively as those facts are announced. These number are added to 60 and bring the total of 73 which corresponds to the addition of the marked dates.

With different months, the key-number varies, so the performer should always add his Sundays before starting the experiment.

3. THE MENTAL NUMBER Tell a person to take an odd number of coins and arrange them in two rows, the rows being equal except for the odd or extra coin. He is then to place the odd coin in the top row.

Now ask the person to name a small number, less than the number of coins in the top row. Suppose he names four. Tell him to take his four coins away from the top row. Next he is to count the coins remaining in the top row and remove *that number* from the bottom row.

By way of illustration, suppose that the person took nineteen coins, arranging them in rows of ten and nine respectively:

1 2 3 4 5 6 7 8 9 10
  1 2 3 4 5 6 7 8 9

Remove *four* from the *top* row leaves him *six* in that row, thus:

1 2 3 4 5 6
  1 2 3 4 5 6 7 8 9

And when he counts that number (six) and removes it from the *bottom* row, the coins will be as follows:

1 2 3 4 5 6
  1 2 3

Now the person is told to take away all the coins remaining in the top row, as you wish to concentrate upon the coins still left in the bottom row:

1 2 3

After due concentration, you name the number correctly: "Three." Yet all during the operation, your back has been turned, and you had no way of even guessing the number of coins involved in the process.

This trick can prove exceedingly baffling to spectators, yet the secret is very simple and the trick is sure-fire if you emphasize each step of the procedure. It all depends on the number that the person decides to take away from the top row, in this instance *four*. You have him announce that number—something that he is later apt to forget he did—and you know then that the final number of coins will be *one less,* in this case *three.*

It will come out just the same no matter how many coins are used at the start and the result will always be one less than the original subtraction, as four—three; three—two; two—one; one—zero. Thus the trick will vary when repeated.

4. THE EQUAL ROWS Similiar in effect to the "Mental Number" but with a distinct difference in procedure and calculation, this trick with equal rows forms a separate mystery in itself.

A person is asked to form two rows of coins, each containing the same number. This is done while the magician's back is turned. We shall suppose that eight coins are placed in each row:

$$1 \quad 2 \quad 3 \quad 4 \quad 5 \quad 6 \quad 7 \quad 8$$
$$1 \quad 2 \quad 3 \quad 4 \quad 5 \quad 6 \quad 7 \quad 8$$

Now the person may take coins away or add them to either row, using more coins if he so desires. He may transfer coins from one row to the other, but always he must state what his action is. For example, suppose he takes three from the top row, puts one in the bottom and eliminates the other two. The rows will then stand:

$$1 \quad 2 \quad 3 \quad 4 \quad 5$$
$$1 \quad 2 \quad 3 \quad 4 \quad 5 \quad 6 \quad 7 \quad 8 \quad 9$$

The magician then tells him to remove the top row entirely, counting the coins in that row. The spectator keeps this number (five) to himself and is then told to take that same number of coins from the bottom row, which will then be:

$$1 \quad 2 \quad 3 \quad 4$$

Thereupon the magician concentrates and names the exact number remaining in the row: "Four."

No matter how complex the spectator tries to make this trick, it still remains simple to the magician, and very much so. All he has to do is *assume* that each row contains eight coins. Every time coins are transferred, added or subtracted, the magician simply follows the process mentally, with eight as his basis.

In the case given, he took three from the top and added one to the bottom, giving him five and nine. He told the person to take away the top row because it was smaller, and therewith the magician mentally subtracted *five* when he told the spectator to take the same number from the bottom row.

That left *four* and the result would have been the same no matter what number was used at the start, provided the two rows were equal.

One very good way to demonstrate this mental marvel is with piles of coins or matches. Let a person do a lot of adding and subtracting, then tell him to take away the "left" or "right" pile according to which is smaller. When he counts the number in that pile to remove the same number from the other, he may not even know the number himself until he has counted it.

Thus when the magician comes through with the final total, the trick will seem like real mind-reading.

5. THREE HEAP MYSTERY For this mental mystery, playing cards are preferable, as they can be dealt in transferring them from one heap to another. However, the trick is applicable to other objects such as chips, coins or matches.

Someone is told to deal three heaps of cards, making them all equal, but using any number that may be desired. He is then asked to name a number between one and ten. This is written on a slip of paper and laid aside.

The person is told to take the left heap and deal three cards from it into the center heap. Then he must take the right heap and from it deal three cards into the center. He counts the number of cards remaining in the right heap (say seven) and is then to pick up the center heap and deal that number (seven) into the left heap.

Assuming that the person chose *nine* as the number that he wrote on the slip of paper. The magician tells him to count the number of cards in the center heap. To his amazement, the spectator finds that he has exactly nine.

The reason is that he will *always* have nine at that point. Suppose that the person began with ten cards in each heap:

$$10 \qquad 10 \qquad 10$$

He deals three from the left heap into the center; then three from the right heap into the center, leaving:

10	10	10
minus	plus	minus
3	6	3

The left and right heaps each contain *seven* cards so when that many is dealt from the center heap, the result will be sixteen less seven—or nine. The 10 simply stands for X, which in this case is an unknown quantity, because the result will always be the same, no matter what number is used as the basis for the original heaps.

All the magician has to do is remember the process and give the instructions. The spectator is then sure to wind up with nine cards in the center heap.

But suppose the spectator has named some other number

as the one he wants for the final result? That's very easy. Knowing the number that was written on the slip of paper, the magician orders the person to do some more dealing to fit the case.

Knowing that the spectator has nine cards in hand, the magician can bring them down to *five*, by telling him to deal two on the left and two on the right. The total can be reduced to *four* by instructing the spectator to pick up one card from either heap, left or right, then deal three cards on the left and three on the right. Any such process will only puzzle the spectator the more.

Used in combination with other dealing or counting tricks, this mystery of the three heaps will always prove highly effective.

6. ADD THE DICE Use two dice for this trick: one red, the other green. While your back is turned, have someone roll the dice. Suppose they come: red 2; green 5.

Without looking at the dice, tell the person to multiply the red by 5 (making 10) and to add the green (making 15). He is to double the total (15 doubled making 30) and then to add 11 (totalling 41). From this he must subtract the green number (5) and name the answer (36).

Immediately you state that the dice showed 2 for the red and 5 for the green. The figures of that total (36) give you the answer. Subtract 1 from the first figure to get the red; one from the second for the green.

This works with any numbers that may be rolled.

7. NAMING THE NUMBER The performer gives a pad and pencil to a person and requests him to write any number of three different figures. Then he is to reverse that number and write the smaller above the larger. Example: 382, reversed, 283.

When this has been done, the performer tells him to draw a line under the numbers and to subtract the smaller from the larger. After he has made the subtraction, the magician concentrates and then names the result.

First we must note a peculiarity that is evident in any subtraction of this type:

The answer will always be one of these numbers: 99, 198, 297, 396, 495, 594, 693, 792, 891. Of these numbers, 198 and 891 are very uncommon.

The performer pays little attention to his subject until the man is making the subtraction. Then the magician watches him from a distance, and notes his hand or the tip of his pencil.

If only two figures are written, the answer is 99. If three figures are written, the performer has only to identify one (except the center figure which is always 9).

This is an extremely easy matter which can be done on the first trial; and after some experience the performer can catch one of the numbers by a mere glance at the proper moment. Yet he is too far away to see the writing on the paper, or he cannot see it because of the elevation of the pad so no one will suspect anything.

Remember that the subtraction is from right to left. The center number is always sure. There is a distinct difference in the movement of the hand when it makes a 2 or a 6, and one figure caught gives the clue to the whole number.

8. BOARDS AND CARDS The magician gives out six envelopes each containing six different playing cards. He asks the persons who receive the envelopes to remember one card each, replacing all the cards in the envelope.

Then the magician holds up a board with six cards attached. He asks each person if he sees his card on the board. If the person says "Yes," the magician immediately names the card, even though he does not see the face of the board.

This is repeated with the remaining boards until the cards have been named. Sometimes two or more persons will have a card on one board, sometimes none.

Each board has one card from each envelope. The envelopes are numbered from 1 to 6. Now these duplicate cards are not definitely arranged on the board—they are there at random, but on the back of the board the magician has a tiny list.

For example: 1—JS; 2—10H; 3—AS; 4—9C; 5—4H; 6—QC.

These abbreviations stand for jack of spades; ten of hearts; ace of spades; nine of clubs; four of hearts; queen of clubs.

Each board is similarly arranged.

The magician picks up any board, and without looking at the front of it, holds the cards towards the spectators.

If the man with envelope 1 says he sees the card he mentally selected, the magician simply notes number 1 on the list and names that card. He does the same with any board and any number.

9. FIVE CARDS AND FIVE PELLETS Five cards chosen by five spectators; and each person receives a slip of paper upon which he writes the name of this card. He rolls the slip into a ball and lays it upon the card, which is face down.

The magician tosses the paper balls into a glass and picks up the five cards. Then he orders the balls to be rolled on the table. At his instruction, four of the persons each pick up a paper ball.

The magician drops one of the cards on the table, and puts the remaining paper ball upon it. When the ball is unrolled, it is read, and we will presume it says "Eight of Clubs". The card is turned up—and it is the eight of clubs!

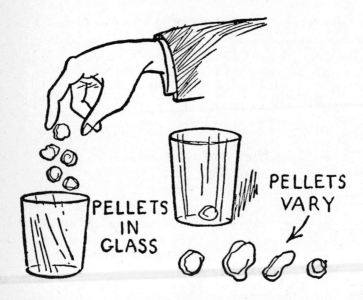

PELLETS
IN
GLASS

PELLETS
VARY

Of course it can be done when all the cards are alike—that's not a bad idea—but in this trick a borrowed pack is used. The secret lies in the paper balls.

First of all, the slips are roughly torn and they vary in size. As no two people will roll a paper ball alike, the result is five different balls, varying slightly in size.

In picking up the cards upon which the balls rest, the magician takes the one with the smallest ball first and so on, following in order of size, or noting any other slight difference in the pellets.

When the balls are rolled from the glass, four of them are picked up, one by one. The magician easily detects which remains—number one, two, three, four or five; and he tosses the corresponding card on the table.

10. THE MYSTERIOUS NAME   This trick is done with a sheet of cigarette paper. The magician rolls the paper into a tiny ball, lays it on the table and asks the spectator to name

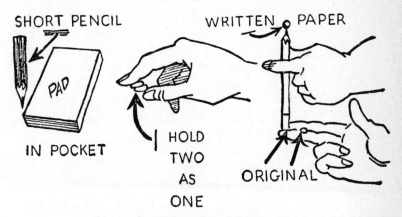

SHORT PENCIL   WRITTEN   PAPER

PAD

IN POCKET   HOLD

TWO

AS   ORIGINAL

ONE

Left: The pad in the pocket.
Center: Exchanging the pellets.
Right: Concealing the original pellet.

some famous person. The paper ball is placed upon the tip of a pencil. When opened, it bears the chosen name.

In his trousers' pocket the magician has a pad of cigarette papers and a very short pencil. When he has rolled up a blank piece of paper he asks for a famous name. The moment it is given, he puts his hand in his pocket and writes the name on top of the pad with the short pencil. He then tears off the slip, rolls it into a wad and conceals it between the tips of his first two fingers.

He brings his hand forth and picks up the slip on the table, adding the other little ball to it. He holds the two as one and turns them over. Everyone supposes that he holds the original ball alone.

In his left hand the magician holds a pencil, point upward. His right fingers retain the original ball of paper, but set the ball with the written name upon the point.

The pencil is of the eraser type, but the rubber is missing. The cavity from which it came is partly filled with wax. The right fingers pass to the bottom of the pencil and it is set upon the hidden ball, which sticks to the wax. With his right hand the magician gives the pencil to a spectator. Then he shows his hands absolutely empty. When the paper ball is opened, the name is written on it—and the magician calmly pockets the pencil!

11. FINGER FANTASY

This is a baffling demonstration of quick mentality that will stand repetition to the point where the witnesses will be almost frantic. The magician turns his back and tells two people each to hold up one hand and display any number of fingers, a closed fist standing for zero.

As soon as the hands are thus shown, someone else is to call the total of the two hands. Immediately the magician names the individual numbers that the two persons have shown. For example, suppose that one player is showing two fingers, the other four. The total of "Six" is announced and the magician states that the first person's number is two, the second person's four.

Obviously this is an excellent guess, since various combinations might have occurred to form the six total. So to

194

prove that more than guess-work is involved, the magician tells the players to lower their hands and raise them again, changing the number of fingers as they wish. Again, when the total is called—say five—the magician gives the individual numbers correctly, for instance: four and one.

A third play follows. A number is called, such as three and the magician announces that the first person is showing one finger, the second person two. Once more the magician is correct and as the play continues, he keeps on hitting the right results every time he hears a total.

The trick is done with the aid of a confederate, Player A, who uses a simple system whereby the magician can name A's number and that of the other player, B. The method is so easy that it can be taught to anyone in a very few minutes.

The system is this: On the first play, the confederate, A, always shows two fingers. Thus when the magician hears the total, he can state A's number, subtract it from the total and give B's. In the example given, A showed two, B showed four. Hence upon hearing six as the total, the magician knew that B was displaying four fingers.

The number shown by B, in this case four, is A's cue for the number that he is to show on the *next* play. Thus on the second play, the magician already knows that A will show four. Hearing a total of five, he knows that B is showing one finger.

For the third play, A uses one as his cue number, so when the total is announced as three, the magician knows that B must be showing two. That number—two—will be A's cue for the next play, and so on.

The totals are announced by a third person, who does all the speaking to the magician. This person can be changed at any time and curiously, any suspicion of confederacy is apt to be directed at that person. Should witnesses suspect the real confederate, A, or for that matter, the innocent party, B, the magician immediately tells the two finger showers to turn back to back.

Neither can then see the number of fingers that the other shows. This has no bearing on the result whatever, because if A happens to be showing three fingers and hears a total of eight, he knows that B is showing five and thus gets his cue for the next play, just as the magician does. But the effect upon the witnesses is remarkable. They think that one player has to try to fake a total by watching what the other does. The business of playing one turn ahead never occurs to anyone.

The only hitch that can occur is when people insist that the players be changed, but the trick should not be continued long enough to allow this. If someone is very anxious to enter the game, let that person replace B, and then conclude the trick after several plays.

Of course there is also the device of having a second confederate handy as a replacement for A, in which case the trick can be continued longer, letting different people play the part of B and finally putting the new stooge in for A. A neat stunt is to bring in the second confederate as B and later dispose of A, whereupon B takes over the business of the cues.

Since the magician is pretending to catch the thoughts of the individual players, A and B, he should state that he needs suitable subjects for the trick, as all minds are not tuned to his vibration. The magician can purposely fail when trying one person as B and therefore put in someone else instead. This will throw suspicion on the player who takes the part of B thereby drawing that same suspicion from the real culprit, A.

196

12. TOTAL FORETOLD

A slip is sealed in an envelope. Single figures are given to the magician who writes them in a column on the face of the envelope. He adds the total and lets someone take the envelope to check it. The envelope is opened. The slip within bears the total that was added on the face of the envelope!

Write any number—say 35—on your slip and seal it in the envelope. Ask for single figures, write them in column form and ADD THEM as you proceed.

Taking 35 as the total you want, 26 (9 less than 35) will be your key. The moment that the figures total 26 or above, stop asking for figures. State that you will draw a line and let the figures be added.

As you proceed to draw the line, hold the face of the envelope to yourself. At the bottom of the column write a figure of your own—the exact figure that is needed to make the total come to 35!

Continue by drawing the line. The whole action is natural—no one will ever suspect what you have done. Pass the envelope and the pencil to a spectator and let him add the total.

13. SPELL YOUR CHOICE

The magician lays some objects on a table. He asks a person to select one mentally and remember it by name. Let us suppose that a pencil is chosen. The magician tells the person to turn his back and wait until the magician says: "Go".

With that word, the magician touches an object. The person mentally spells the first letter in the name of the selected object. In this case, he would repeat the letter "P" to himself.

The magician touches another object and says: "Go," for the second time. The person mentally declares the second letter, in this case "E". This is repeated, with the understanding that after the person has spelled the last letter in his word, he must call "Stop" and turn around.

Reaching "L" in pencil, the person says: "Stop." He looks around. To his surprise, the magician is touching the pencil, and all the witnesses testify to the fact that he had his hand on that object when the chooser called: "Stop."

The trick works automatically, provided you choose the proper objects. These must be items that are each spelled with a different number of letters. For instance:

PIN	Three letters
DIME (or COIN)	Four letters
WATCH	Five letters
PENCIL	Six letters
PICTURE	Seven letters
ENVELOPE	Eight letters
CIGARETTE	Nine letters
FLASHLIGHT	Ten letters
HANDKERCHIEF	Twelve letters

When you first say: "Go", place your finger on any object. Do the same on the second count. On the third, however, touch the pin. If the person has chosen the pin, his mental spelling ends there, for "pin" has three letters.

Touch the coin for four, the watch for five, and so on. Whatever object has been chosen, the spelling must end with it. Notice that the list contains no word with eleven letters. If the count goes that high, simply touch any object for eleven —but touch the handkerchief for twelve.

14. FIVE CARD MYSTERY Showing five playing cards in a fan, the magician asks someone to think of a single card in the group and keep repeating the name of the card to himself, but not aloud, as this is purely an effort at mental concentration.

The person then writes down the name of the card without the magician seeing it. Meanwhile the magician places the five cards in his pocket. Now, concentrating deeply, the magician draws out four cards and lays them face down on the table or places them in the spectator's hand.

The paper is opened; the name of the card is read aloud: say the six of spades. Reaching in his pocket, the magician brings out the fifth and last card and shows it to be that very card, the six of spades. The cards on the table are turned face up while the magician is bringing the last card from his pocket and since the six of spades is not among them, it naturally is the card the magician kept. But the question is, how did he know to keep it—unless he actually read the spectator's thought!

No thought reading is involved. In his pocket, the magician has four other cards. The five cards that he originally shows consist of a five spot, a six, a seven, an eight and a nine. He arranges them in numerical order when he puts them into his pocket.

When he brings out four cards, they are the extras that were in his pocket beforehand. Now, whatever the spectator's mental choice, the magician learns it when the paper is unfolded. He then reaches into his pocket and counts to himself: Five, six, seven, eight, nine—a card for each count—and he brings out the card as named on the paper.

Very good, but the trick would seem to have one flaw. Those four cards on the table are *not* members of the original group. How then can they be turned face up, without somebody recognizing that an exchange has been made?

That is the very subtle feature of this trick, the point that makes it a real mystery. Assuming that the five original cards are the Five of Clubs, Six of Spades, Seven of Spades, Eight of Clubs, and Nine of Spades, it will be noted that the cards are all quite similar. Told to concentrate on *one card* and remember it, the spectator will not bother with the others, nor will any other observers remember them as anything except a batch of black spot cards.

The four extra cards that the performer has in his pocket should then be the Five of Spades, Seven of Clubs, Eight of Spades and Nine of Clubs. These cards closely resemble the four that the magician is sure to leave in his pocket; hence when they are turned up later, they will be accepted as members of the original group.

Turning up the cards is very helpful, because people take it for granted that they are four originals even before the magician brings the chosen card from his pocket. The fact that people are looking at those cards during the pocket count, will make the trick all the easier.

Chapter 13

SPECIAL CARD TRICKS

HERE ARE CARD TRICKS THAT REQUIRE SPECIAL ARRANGE-
ments, slight preparation, or the use of an extra pack of
cards—factors which put these particular tricks somewhat out
of the impromptu category. Also included in this chapter are
tricks requiring special practice or the services of an assistant.

This does not detract from such tricks; quite to the contrary. Through a set-up or some other arrangement, it is
possible to gain results beyond those of the average card trick,
so the performer should take advantage of this whenever
feasible.

There is nothing suspicious about a magician bringing out
his own pack of cards, provided it is of a common pattern and
can be handled by the audience as he proceeds with his tricks.
Being a magician, he would naturally carry a pack on the
chance that he might not be able to borrow one.

That of course gives the magician an advantage with his
opening trick and he will find some excellent material for that
purpose in this chapter. Also it is often possible to "set" a
borrowed pack between tricks. Always a magician should take
advantage of such opportunity. In fact he should take ad-

vantage of all opportunities, because that is part of the business of being a magician.

1. THE TEN CARD CIRCLE This trick is simple but puzzling. It is described here in detail for two reasons: First, because it is a good impromptu trick in this form; second, because the trick which follows is a great improvement that will be more readily understood when one knows the circle method.

The cards, numbered from ace to ten, are arranged faces up like the circle of a clock dial. A spectator is invited to *think* of one card. Another person is asked to *point out* one card. Suppose, for instance, that the eight is thought of and the five is pointed out.

Noting the five, the magician adds ten, and says: "I want you—" the spectator who is thinking of the card—"to count from the five spot. Begin the count with your own number and count to fifteen, moving to the left."

The spectator does this. He places his finger on the five and says "eight"; he touches the four and says "nine"; he continues in this manner and when he reaches fifteen—the number set by the magician—he is astonished to find that his count has ended on the very card he chose, the eight spot!

This trick always works. Simply follow the system as described and the result will be the same. Remember to add ten to the number indicated.

To make the trick more perplexing, it is wise to use cards of different suits, but in numerical order, and to lay them faces down. Let a person peek at one card while your back is turned. Another person points out a card at random and turns it face up. Add ten to its value, tell the thinker to start his count at that card, and to begin with his own number. The fact

202

that he arrives on his own card which is face down makes the experiment doubly preplexing.

2. DEAL THE NUMBER   A pack is shuffled. Ten cards are dealt off by a spectator. He notes the position of any card from the bottom of the heap—say six of clubs, four from the bottom.

The magician takes the heap. He asks someone to name a number below ten. Take eight, for instance. The magician removes eight cards from the bottom of the packet, saying: "Eight and ten make eighteen. We will count to eighteen beginning with your number," pointing to the person who is thinking of the fourth card from the bottom.

The person says his number is four. The magician deals a card, counting "four". He does not drop the card to the table. He puts it under the heap from which he is dealing. He repeats this with the next cards, counting "five, six" and so on, thus he has an inexhaustible heap from which to deal. When he reaches eighteen, the number which he designated, the spectator's thought-of card is the one that he turns up. If he wishes, the performer can let the spectator do the dealing in the fashion described, counting to himself and ending on the mentally selected card. That is a good method to use as a repeat.

Keep these points in mind: the card mentally selected is noted counting from the *bottom* of the packet. The number of cards named by the second spectator are shifted in a group from bottom to top. The deal is made from the top, with the cards faces down, the cards going to the bottom one by one. The final card is turned up.

3. A MYSTIC PREDICTION   In this trick, the magician volunteers to make a remarkable prediction. He writes something upon a sheet of paper and folds it. He removes a pack of cards from its case and puts the folded paper therein. He arranges some cards in five heaps which lie in a row upon the table. He remarks that these heaps may be counted singly, from left to right.

A person is requested to select a heap, the magician making it plain that the heap selected will be the one used. "Take any heap," are his words, "and you will discover that I have foretold the very heap which you chance to choose!"

A heap is designated. The paper is taken from the card case. It is opened. It bears the words: "You choose the five heap." This prediction is verified. The magician proves unmistakably that the chooser has taken the "five" heap.

The important secret of this experiment is that any one of the heaps will fill the bill. Each can be made to pass as the so-called "five" heap. This depends upon the arrangement of the cards.

One heap consists of all the five-spots. Should it be chosen, the magician turns it face upward and shows that it has four fives. He shows the faces of the other cards. There are no fives among them. If this heap is taken, the magician says: "This, you see, is the 'five' heap—all five-spots."

Another heap contains exactly five cards. It is the only heap which has that number; all other heaps have either more or less than five cards. Should this particular heap be selected, the wizard says:

"The 'five' heap. Your heap is the only one with five cards." He counts the cards in that heap and also the cards in the other heaps. But he turns none of the heaps face upward. This artifice is very convincing.

A third heap can also be made to appear as the "five" heap. It contains just four cards—three aces and a two-spot. If this

204

heap is selected, the magician picks it up and holds it face downward. One by one, he deals the cards face up on the table, counting the spots: "One, two, three, and two make five!"

He then deals the other heaps the same way, showing that each has cards totalling more than five. When he picks up the heap with four fives, he simply deals two cards face up saying: "Five—ten—that's more than five already!"

When these heaps are laid out, the heap with the four fives should be in the center, flanked by the other two heaps just mentioned, the magician knowing the position of each individual heap. There are two more heaps to consider. These are the end heaps. Each consist of eight or nine indifferent cards.

Should one of these heaps be designated, the magician tells the chooser to leave it on the table. The paper is opened. The message is read.

"The 'five' heap," says the magician. "I told you that we count the heaps one, two, three, four, five—from left to right. That makes your heap number five—the 'five' heap."

It makes no difference which end heap is chosen. If the one selected is at the performer's right, he counts the heaps himself, running his hand from left to right. If the selected heap is at the performer's left, he orders the chooser to count to the correct heap—one, two, three, four, five—and the count ends on the selected heap.

It is advisable to call for this counting before the message is read. That makes the choice unmistakably five and the spectator picks up the heap while the paper is being unfolded. The magician then sweeps the other four heaps together and replaces them with the pack.

By having these cards set in order in the pack, the trick

may be presented in a very smart fashion. It is a great improvement on old ideas of this order and can be turned into a very puzzling problem. It depends entirely upon presentation and requires no skill whatever.

4. DOUBLE DISCOVERY   A person takes a pack of cards from the performer. He cuts it in two heaps. He removes a cluster of cards from the lower half. He counts those cards and notes the bottom card of the group—say seven cards with the six of spades on the bottom. He must not take more than thirteen cards.

He is instructed to place the group with the chosen card on the other half of the pack. The performer's back is turned while this goes on. When the operation is completed, the magician turns around and picks up the pack, putting the top half on top.

Now he deals cards faces down, in a sort of a circle. He does this with about twenty cards. Running his hand around, he suddenly turns a card face up. It is a seven-spot. The performer announces that there were seven cards in the spectator's group. Instantly, the performer turns up another card. It is the six of spades, the card noted by the person.

In doing this trick, the magician first states that jack counts as eleven, queen as twelve and king as thirteen. On top of the pack he has thirteen cards arranged in this order, from the top: king, queen, jack, ten, nine, eight, seven, six, five, four, three, two, ace.

Note that the group taken by the spectator goes on these cards. It does not matter how many cards the group contains. The fourteenth card from the top will indicate, by its value, the number of cards put on by the spectator.

Thus the spectator takes seven cards, the bottom of his

group being the six of spades, which he remembers. The performer deals from fifteen to twenty cards in a rough circle. He turns up the fourteenth card, counting around the circle and it is a seven-spot.

That gives him a clue to the location of the spectator's noted card. It must be the one that was dealt seventh in the circle. Quickly going around the circle, the magician turns up the seventh card to reveal it as the selected one.

Suppose the spectator had ten cards in his group, with the five of clubs on the bottom. The fourteenth card, when turned up by the conjuror, would be a ten-spot. Counting to the tenth card in the circle, the performer would discover the five of clubs.

Immediately after revealing the selected card, the magician should mix the cards of the circle as he prepares to gather them up. This destroys any arrangement and leaves the spectators wondering, even if they do happen to see the faces of the cards.

5. THE CARD FORETOLD There are various card tricks that involve predictions; this is one of the simplest yet most effective. It may be performed with an ordinary pack although the magician must be set beforehand.

A pack of cards is divided into two heaps which are shuffled together in dovetail fashion—a careful, legitimate shuffle. Something is written on a sheet of paper which is dropped in a glass or placed in the card-case.

Turning the pack face up, the magician states that he will carefully separate the reds from the blacks. Someone else may do this if desired—but the magician requests that it be done exactly, dealing each red or black card as it comes.

Thus two piles are obtained. A person is asked to choose

either the red heap or the black heap. Suppose red is taken. The magician gives the cards value from one to thirteen— ace, one; jack, eleven; queen, twelve; king, thirteen. He asks all to note that if two cards are taken from the red heap, their value may indicate any number from one to twenty-six: two aces equalling two; two kings, twenty-six; other pairs, numbers in between. This fact is readily understood.

So the magician asks the spectator to cut the red pack at any point and to add the values of the two cards above and below the cut. These two values are to designate a card in the black heap—counting down from the top.

The cut is made. We will suppose that a five and a nine appear. They total fourteen. A spectator counts down fourteen in the black heap. The card is the ace of clubs. The folded paper is opened. It bears the name "ace of clubs"!

Now for the simple method. The magician first separates the red cards from the blacks—long before he shows the trick. He arranges the red cards thus:

King, ace, queen, two, jack, three, ten, four, nine, five, eight, six, seven, seven, eight, six, nine, five, ten, four, jack, three, queen, two, king, ace.

There is no arrangement of the black heap. The magician simply notes the fourteenth card from the bottom. That is the card upon which the choice is to fall—in this instance, the ace of clubs.

When the pack is introduced, the two heaps are segregated as described—one color being upon the other. The magician turns the faces of the cards toward himself; spreading them slightly, he separates the pack so that he has the reds in one hand and the blacks in the other. He then proceeds with the dovetail shuffle—or lets some spectator perform that action.

The Result: Reds and blacks are intermingled, but the reds still retain their original order and the ace of clubs is still fourteen from the bottom—among the blacks. So when the pack is turned face up and the cards are separated one by one into two heaps, the peculiar arrangement of the reds remains comparatively the same. The ace of clubs now becomes fourteen from the top in the black heap.

The arrangement of the reds is important for this reason: no matter where that heap is cut, the cards above and below the cut will add to a total of either thirteen or fourteen! If the total is thirteen, the magician asks someone to remove thirteen cards from the top of the black heap and to look at the next card. If the total is fourteen, he tells the person to look at the fourteenth card from the top of the black heap. In either instance, the action seems to abide by the magician's promise to take the card at the number designated by the red totals. Also, in either instance, the card consulted is the ace of clubs.

The magician has, of course, written his mysterious words early in the trick, just after introducing the pack. So everyone is due for amazement when the paper is opened and seen to bear the words "ace of clubs."

There is just one other point. The magician, after the cards are separated, allows the spectator to select either heap, reds or blacks. This is simply a bit of by-play. Since both heaps are to be used, the magician cannot go wrong. If reds are taken, he uses them to ascertain a number in the black heap. If blacks are taken, he states that he has predicted a black card and merely uses the red heap to pick a number at random.

6. PASSE PASSE CARDS Two packs of cards are used in this trick, preferably a red pack and a blue pack. Also two drinking glasses (stands if giant cards are used) and some rubber bands.

Taking the red pack of cards, the magician has one selected. It is replaced in a cluster of about twelve cards which the magician removes from the bottom of the deck. Encircled with rubber bands, this packet is placed in a glass.

Next a card is similarly taken from the blue pack and is replaced in a cluster of about twelve cards taken from the bottom of the pack. This group is also girded with rubber bands and it goes in the other glass.

To show the location of each heap, a card is removed from each group and set back forward in front of the glass in which the group is located. On the right, a red card shows the red packet; on the left, a blue card shows the blue packet.

The magician takes both packets, explaining that the rubber bands now make it impossible to remove a card from the group without considerable difficulty. He tosses the groups in the air. He picks them up or catches them. He puts the red group in its glass, the blue group in the other. Now comes the baffling finish. The glasses are given to the spectators. Among the red cards is found the blue-backed card that was selected from the blue pack! Among the blue cards is discovered the red-backed card that was taken from the red pack!

A wonderful trick, yet quite simple and easy to do. Just a bit of quick preparation is necessary. Before performing, take one dozen red cards from the red pack and put them on the bottom of the blue pack. Likewise take a dozen blue cards and put them on the bottom of the red pack.

Important: The bottom card of each group should be the same—say, the six of diamonds. Then the performer is ready to work. If he is using his own cards, he should have the packs in their cases.

A card is chosen from the red pack. In spreading the pack for a selection, the magician does not spread the bottom cards.

Hence the blue backs do not come into view. After the card is taken, the magician spreads the faces of the pack toward the spectators. This enables him to see the backs. He draws off all the blue cards from the bottom, but keeps one red card on

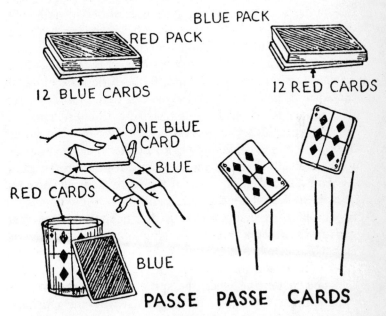

Arrangement of packs and various stages in the Passe Passe Card Trick.

top of them. He squares these cards and holds them faces down for the insertion of the chosen card. The single red-backed card makes it seem as though the group consisted entirely of red-backed cards.

The procedure with the blue pack is exactly the same. The red-backed cards at the bottom are not spread when a blue card is selected. But in spreading the pack faces front, the red-backed cards are drawn off beneath a blue-backed card.

The chosen blue card goes into the little squared-up heap. It appears to be going into a packet of bona fide blue cards.

Each packet is girded with rubber bands and placed in a glass, with the bottom card facing the audience. To point out the location of red and blue, the magician takes the top card from each heap and sets it in front of the glass. This is a clever idea. It disposes of the extra card in each group.

One packet is taken in each hand, faces of the cards toward the audience. Each packet appears the same, because the facing cards are identical. Each is a six of diamonds. Now the groups are brought together and tossed. When they come down, no one knows which is which. But the magician shows the backs and calmly places the red-backed group in the glass indicated by the red card, while the blue-backed packet goes in the glass indicated by the blue card.

No one realizes the subtle change that has taken place. Yet the performer announces that the simple toss in the air has caused each selected card to leave its own group and pass into the other! Wonderful, if true.

It appears to be true when the spectators take the packets from the glasses. The blue-backed card is with the reds; the red-backed card is in the midst of the blues. Not a clue to the secret remains.

7. CARDS AND ENVELOPES A very surprising mystery. Three selected cards apparently leave an envelope and pass into a group of cards contained in another envelope.

The magician begins by dealing sixteen cards from a pack. These sixteen cards are counted by a spectator. The magician puts them in an envelope, which is sealed and marked.

Next, sixteen more cards are counted faces down; they are spread on the table and three cards are turned up and noted by spectators. The magician shuffles these cards and puts them in the second envelope, which is also sealed.

The first surprise comes when nineteen cards are discovered in the first envelope. Opening the second envelope and count ing the cards therein, only thirteen are found. Then the nineteen group is counted faces up and the chosen cards are discovered in it!

The secret depends upon two groups of sixteen cards that are exactly alike. This means that the magician must use his own pack, having his special arrangement made up with the aid of a duplicate pack. The groups of sixteen cards are on top of the pack. Thus when the magician counts off sixteen cards and then another group of sixteen, he is forming two heaps that are identical. But the cards are faces down so no one knows this fact.

Beneath one envelope, which we will call A, are three odd cards, lying faces down. The envelope and the cards overlap the edge of the table slightly. Now, the performer must secretly add those three cards to the sixteen which he intends to put into envelope A.

There are two ways of doing this. First method Lay the sixteen cards faces down on the envelope, drawing out the envelope at almost the same moment. Second method: Pick up the envelope with the three cards beneath it and let it rest momentarily above the sixteen cards. The three odd cards are allowed to fall upon the sixteen, which are a trifle disarranged.

Either method works and the upshot is that nineteen cards go into envelope A, despite the fact that sixteen were carefully counted at the outset.

Three cards are now selected from the other group—the cards that are to go into envelope B. Note that these cards are turned up from among the sixteen, so no one becomes acquainted with any of the cards other than the selected ones.

Upon shuffling this bunch of sixteen, the magican holds the group in his right hand, thumb at one end, fingers at the other —the cards faces down beneath the hand. With the aid of the left hand, he forms a slight space at the bottom of the group so that three cards are detached from the others.

He picks up envelope B and holds it with the flap extended, and the face of the envelope downward. He moves the envelope toward his right hand, the extended flap pointing like an arrow.

In sliding the cards into the envelope, it is a simple matter to insert the point of the flap between the bulk of thirteen cards and the three odd cards that are separated beneath. The result is that only thirteen cards actually go into envelope B. The rest go beneath. The left fingers, under the envelope, help the odd cards into position and hold them there.

This envelope is held momentarily over the pack of cards, which is lying, somewhat disarranged, on the table. The left fingers release their cards, so that the odd cards fall on the table. Envelope B is then sealed.

Now for the action, the important part of the trick being ended. The performer commands the selected cards to pass from envelope B to envelope A. Upon opening envelope A, nineteen cards are discovered, being counted faces down. Envelope B is opened. Only thirteen cards, counted faces down.

Picking up the pack, the performer holds it in his left hand, while the right holds the thirteen cards. Spectators are told to turn the nineteen cards faces up and look for the three selected cards. During this search, the magician adds the three top

214

cards of the pack to the thirteen in his right hand and transfers all to the bottom of the pack. He quietly counts off thirteen, to be ready in case anyone asks to see the thirteen cards from envelope B.

To make this quick, those thirteen cards can be previously bent upward in the center so they can be lifted off the pack when needed. Generally the spectators are so surprised to find the chosen cards with the nineteen that the trick can be ended there. Due to the duplication of the packets, the selected cards must be in the nineteen heap.

8. POCKET TO POCKET Have a person cut a pack of cards. Let him count the cards in his heap. Suppose there are twenty-four. That leaves twenty-eight with you, as you verify by counting. For there are fifty-two cards in a pack.

Give the person your heap and let him put it in his inside pocket. Take his heap and put it in your inside pocket. Presto! Three cards leave his pocket and come into yours. He finds that his stock of twenty-eight is reduced to twenty-five, while you now have twenty-seven instead of twenty-four.

Anyone can count the cards when they are brought from the pockets. Absolutely no deception, so it seems. Especially as a borrowed pack is used.

This is the way. Before starting the trick, smuggle three cards from the pack and put them in your pocket. Let a person take part of the pack, count it, and give it to you—twenty-four cards for example. Meanwhile you count yours as three more than are really there, using the "false count." This is not absolutely necessary as you deduct from fifty-two, but it adds to the effect and as you are merely counting as a matter of routine, no one watches you closely.

Your cards really go into his pocket, three short. His go into your pocket and there they join the three cards that are awaiting them. The trick is as good as done.

9. A FOUR ACE TRICK This is an effective version of the four ace trick, aided by the use of four special envelopes. The magician exhibits the four aces. He deals them in a row on the table. He adds three cards to each ace. He puts each group in an envelope, each envelope having an open front, so the center of the ace is visible.

At the magician's command, all the aces gather in one envelope, leaving four indifferent cards in each of the other envelopes.

The Method: When the four aces are first shown, they are held in a fan. Behind the last ace are three cards, bunched together. When the aces are laid on the pack and redealt in a row, only one of the cards is really an ace. Note that the uppermost of the real aces should be the ace of spades. The hidden cards are the five of diamonds, five of clubs, and three of hearts.

Another system of adding the three indifferent cards is to have them lying face up beneath the envelopes. The magician starts to remove the envelopes and lays down the fan of aces at the same time, covering the three extra cards. Then the cards are closed and dropped faces down on the pack.

With a row of four cards, apparently aces, but only the ace of spades, on the table, the magician deals the three genuine aces on the ace of spades. Then three indifferent cards are placed on each of the supposed aces, twelve cards in all. The packets are now inserted in the envelopes. The open-cut sides of the envelopes are underneath. So when the packets are in the envelopes, the magician can turn over the envelopes and apparently show an ace in each one. The center spots of the fives and the three look like the single spots of the aces.

The envelopes are inverted again and laid in a square, one envelope at each corner. The magician calls for a number: "one, two, three or four." Whatever is given, he counts around the square to the ace of spades. He can start his count wherever he wants, so it does not matter what number is given!

After "selecting" the ace of spades in this fashion, the magician gives that envelope into the keeping of a spectator. Removing the cards from one envelope, he shuffles them, spreads them and shows that the ace is missing. He does the same with each of the other envelopes. At the finish, all four aces are discovered in the envelope which is held by the spectator.

This routine can be performed without the envelopes, but it is not nearly so convincing. The use of the special envelopes, which are easily made, adds much to the trick. The envelopes should be slightly larger than a playing card. Envelopes that open at the end are the best.

10. THE KNIFE IN THE PACK This is a new trick—a very clever effect. Holding a pack horizontally between the tips of his left thumb and forefinger, the magician inserts a knife into the center of the pack.

He immediately announces the name of the card above the knife. He places his right forefinger on top of the pack and lifts up all the cards above the knife, showing the card he named.

The trick may be repeated; and spectators may insert the knife. But the performer, before he lifts the cards will always name the card correctly.

The Method: Use a table-knife with a bright blade. When

the knife has been inserted, tilt the pack very slightly to the right. At the same instant, tilt the knife blade slightly to the left, moving it so that it comes directly under the inner left corner of the pack. You will immediately catch a reflection of the index corner of the card above the knife. That is the card you name, before you lift up the upper half of the pack.

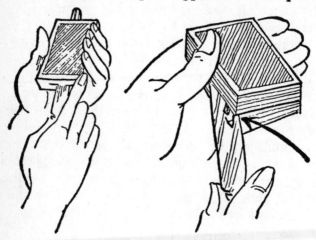

If the pack is held high, so that it is almost on a level with the eyes, the tilting motions are unnecessary. The weight of the knife will bend down the lower half of the cards a bit, and you will catch the reflection easily.

With practice, this trick can be accomplished easily, and with regular precision.

11. THE SPECTATORS' TRICK The ambition of every magician is to allow a spectator to shuffle a pack, and have another person take a card from it and replace it, shuffling the pack for himself—after which the magician finds the chosen card.

This seeming miracle of card magic is quite possible, with the use of a "one way" pack—or "single enders" as they are sometimes termed. Such a pack consists of cards which have a design on the back that is different at one end from the other. Obviously, if the cards are arranged with the patterns all one way, a card that is turned around can be easily discovered by looking through the pack.

Armed with such a pack, with the cards all pointing in one direction, the trick may be undertaken. Let a spectator shuffle the cards—taking care that he does not "riffle" the ends together, but merely uses the ordinary overhand shuffle. Then tell him to spread the cards and let a person take one.

While the pack is still held, tell him to turn his back so that the chooser may insert his card without anyone seeing where it goes. This automatically turns the ends of the cards the other way; so when the chosen card is inserted, the pack may be shuffled normally; yet the magician can immediately find the card by looking through the pack for the one that is reversed.

12. DO AS I DO   This is a trick that lives up to its title in a most astonishing way. Using two packs of cards, the magician and a spectator each select a random card from the different decks, but afterward their choice proves to be identical. Yet all it requires for successful performance is a careful adherence to detail.

The procedure is as follows:

Introducing two packs of cards, the magician invites a spectator to choose one pack. Taking the other deck, the magician shuffles it, saying to the spectator: "Do as I do." So in his turn, the spectator shuffles his own pack.

Now the packs are exchanged, so that each person shuffles

the other's pack. Each pack is then taken back by its original owner. Setting his pack on the table, the magician again says: "Do as I do." Lifting about two-thirds of his pack, he places the larger heap to the right of the smaller. He then takes about half of the larger heap and places it further to the right.

The spectator copies these maneuvers with his own pack. The result: Both the magician and the spectator have three heaps of cards resting on the table. Pointing to his center heap, the magician announces that he will look at the top card of the heap. The spectator is to do the same with the top card of his middle heap. Each card, being noted and remembered, is replaced; but neither the performer nor the assistant show their cards to each other.

Lifting the heap on his left, the magician puts it on the center heap. Lifting both heaps, he places them on the heap at the right. The spectator copies these movements exactly; hence each has definitely looked at a random card and buried it somewhere in the pack. In order to make the cards untraceable, the magician gives his own pack several cuts and the helper copies the process.

Handing his pack to the spectator, the magician takes the latter's pack and states: "I will look for my card in your pack; you look for your card in my pack. When we find our cards, we will lay them face down on the table." To find his card, the magician runs through the faces of the pack and the spectator does the same. Soon the cards are found and are laid face down, side by side. Picking up one card, the magician uses it to flip the other over; then turns up the card he holds.

Magician and spectator have each chosen exactly the same card!

The simple secret of this trick is artfully covered by the elaborate procedure. In shuffling the spectator's pack, the magician finds an opportunity to glance at its bottom card. Thus when the spectator cuts the pack into three heaps as described, looks at the top card of the middle heap and places the left-hand heap upon it, the card known to the magician comes right above the card that the spectator noted.

Cutting the pack does not disturb this pair. When the packs are exchanged again, the magician merely looks for the key card at which he glanced and removes the card just beneath it, as if it were the card he supposedly chose. Since the spectator is removing his own card from the magician's pack, the two are bound to be identical.

13. CARD IN THE POCKET The effect of this trick is that the spectator takes the pack and counts down any number of cards, noting the name of any card and its number from the top of the pack.

The magician returns and receives the pack. Glancing through it, he removes and pockets a card. He asks the spectator's number—not the card. The number being given, the magician counts down that far. The spectator's card is not there, so the magician obligingly removes it from his pocket.

There are several methods of performing this trick. They are given herewith, so that the performer can vary them and thus repeat the trick effectively.

First Method: The performer takes a card from near the bottom of the pack and pockets it. He palms it in his pocket and adds it to the pack when he brings his hand from the pocket.

When the location of the card is given, the wizard counts to it and naturally he stops one short, due to the secretly added card. Suppose the chosen card to be ninth from the top. When he reaches nine, the performer deals the card face down on

221

the table, with the others. It is really the eighth card. Looking at it, the spectator finds that it is not his card.

Meanwhile the performer, just as attention is on the card on the table, palms the real ninth card. Going to his pocket he brings it forth—apparently the card that he put there beforehand.

Second Method: In this variation of the trick, the performer puts the top card in his pocket and leaves it there. Suppose the number is nine. He counts off nine cards with his right hand, each card on the one before, so that their order is reversed. He pushes the next card (really the tenth) from the pack and replaces the right hand cards on the pack.

The spectators look at the card on the table and see that it is not the chosen one. Meanwhile the performer palms the card now on top of the pack, reaches in his pocket and brings it out showing it to be the chosen card. He leaves the odd card in his pocket, later replacing it in the pack.

Third Method: In this version, the performer secretly notes the top card of the pack.* He tells the spectator to deal off any number, one by one; to look at the next card and put the dealt cards on top.

For instance, the spectator deals off eight, looks at the ninth and puts the eighth back on again. The magician returns and looks through the pack for the top card. It is now at number eight, due to the reversal. He takes the card below it (the ninth) and pockets it.

He asks the number. He is told nine. He deals off nine and shows the last one. Not the chosen card. Out it comes from the pocket. This method eliminates the palming.

Fourth Method: Here the performer gives a spectator a slip of paper and tells him to write down any three figures—all

*By means of the "glimpse"—third method.

different—forming a number. He is then to reverse the number and subtract the smaller from the larger.

This being done, add the figures in the result and look at the card that number from the top of the pack. The pack is first shuffled by the spectator.

The secret is the fact that the result will always be 18.

Examples:

451	603	812	594
—154	—306	—218	—495
297	297	594	99

In each case the figures of the result (297, 594, 99) total 18. Knowing this, the magician simply runs down to the eighteenth card and puts it in his pocket, performing the rest of the trick in the accustomed fashion of asking for the number, counting down to it and showing that the chosen card is gone.

Fifth Method: In this version, the magician introduces a pair of dice. He tells someone to roll them and note the total; to pick up one of the dice, add the bottom side and roll it again, adding the new number that turns up. The dice are left on the table. The total is remembered and the card at that number in the pack is the one noted.

The magician, on returning, rolls the dice a few times as though that had some important value. He looks through the pack and puts a card in his pocket. On counting down, the chosen card is missing. It is the one he took.

Simply add seven to the dice as they lie. Thus three and two are rolled—five. The two is turned over; its under side is a five—adding makes ten. The die is rolled again and turns up four. Total, fourteen. The fourteenth card is noted.

When the magician views the dice, he notes four and three.

He adds seven to that total, arriving at fourteen. This gives him the position of the card—fourteenth.

The trick with the dice depends on the fact that opposite sides of a single die always total seven. Yet even people who know it will be fooled by the peculiar way in which the dice are rolled.

Summary: By employing the various methods of performing the card in the pocket, the magician can repeat the trick a number of times or exhibit it differently each time he is requested to perform it.

14. FOUR ACE CHANGE
This is where the laugh is turned on the audience. The magician holds the pack between his hands and shows the ace of clubs on the bottom. He deals the ace face downward. He then puts the next card on top of the pack.

He shows the ace of hearts, the ace of diamonds and the ace of spades, dealing each one and putting the alternate cards on top.

But by this time the spectators know that he is bluffing. For the magician has been showing three spots instead of aces, covering the end spots with his fingers. He has not only done it crudely; he has given it away with the ace of spades. For instead of appearing with a large, ornamental ace, that ace has been shown as only a small spot.

When the magician states that he will transform the aces into threes, everyone demands to see the aces. So the magician obligingly turns them faces up and shows that they are actually aces after all.

That turns the laugh. When the magician decides to go on with the trick, he pushes the cards around a bit, turns them faces up and shows that they are now threes.

Here is the method. The bottom card is really a three; then comes an ace, a three, an ace, a three, an ace, a three (spades) and an ace.

Showing the first three with the fingers covering the end spots, the magician announces that he will deal it on the table. Actually, he uses the "glide"* drawing back the card and dealing an ace in its stead. He transfers the three spot to the top of the pack without showing its face.

He continues thus, showing each three in turn, but really dealing aces. So at last, he has four aces on the table while the threes have been transferred to the top of the pack, each in its proper turn.

The magician then turns up the aces after a long protest has been registered by the audience. At this point he acts as though the trick is ended, with the joke being turned on the spectators.

But he really takes advantage of the situation to exchange the aces for the threes. This is done by the "bottom change"— a sleight fully described in Blackstone's "Modern Card Tricks and Secrets of Magic." It is given briefly here, as in this case the sleight can be done very slowly, for the audience does not know that anything else is coming.

The left thumb, on top of the pack, has pushed the four top cards well to the left. The right hand picks up the aces and holds them faces down, between the first and second fingers. The right hand approaches the left. The lower fingers of the left hand open to receive the aces. The right hand removes the threes between the thumb and forefinger. These cards are immediately dropped on the table.

The magician can then show the cards as threes when he wishes. There is an interesting bit of by-play, however, that adds to the effect of the trick. Moving the cards around, the

*A sleight explained in Chapter Three.

magician peeks at the faces and selects the three of diamonds. He uses it as an indicator to point at the others—without revealing the face of the card.

"It's a funny thing," he remarks. "You thought these aces were other cards, didn't you? What's that? You thought they were the threes! Take this ace of diamonds, for instance. Look at it—you thought it was a three—"

So saying, he skims the ace upward in the air, by holding it between his two first fingers, and twirling it edgewise. As the spectators look upward at the spinning card, it actually appears to be an ace, for the end spots merge with the center one.

When the card strikes the floor, it proves to be a three spot after all. The magician then invites an inspection of the other three cards that are on the table. They, like the diamond, are threes instead of aces.

The success of this trick depends largely upon showmanship and the performer who practices it to gain effect will find that it is a most excellent deception.

15. THREE CARD MONTE   This is a very clever version of the three card monte trick, which can be acquired with little practice and is quite deceptive.

The magician holds three cards in a fan—faces toward the audience. One card is behind the other two—that is the center card of the fan, which we will assume to be the ace of spades.

The magician calls attention to the position of the ace of spades, which is flanked by the ace of hearts and the ace of clubs. He turns the cards faces downward and asks someone to remove the ace of spades. Naturally, the person takes the center card. Imagine his surprise when he discovers that he is holding the ace of hearts instead of the ace of spades!

There is a little sleight used in this trick. Note the position of the cards. The ace of hearts is the front one; the ace of clubs next; the ace of spades behind the other two, peering from between them.

When the cards are turned face down, the right thumb, which is behind the three cards, moves to the right, swinging the ace of spades to the right position. The center card is now

THREE CARD MONTE

How the center ace is shifted secretly to the right. The right thumb performs the action.

the ace of hearts. A person naturally takes it as the ace of spades. The swing of the arm completely covers the sliding of the ace of spades to the right and the spectator has no idea that a change has been made.

16. THE TRAVELING ACE   This follows the "three card monte" that was just explained. It is an old trick, utilized to a new purpose. The reader will recall that the three cards used in the "monte" were the aces of clubs, spades and hearts. There was a reason.

After demonstrating that the ace of hearts mysteriously takes the place of the ace of spades, the performer kindly consents to do the trick again. He turns his back for a moment,

227

while he arranges the cards. He says that he will use the ace of diamonds. Actually, he has the ace of diamonds in his pocket. He uses the ace of hearts to appear as the ace of diamonds.

This time, the red ace is the back card. In setting it behind the angle formed by the other two aces, the wizard fixes matters so that only the point of the heart is visible—thus the card appears as the ace of diamonds.

The reader will remember that in the "monte" trick, the spectators got the ace of hearts instead of the ace of spades. The performer, now showing the three cards, tells them he will make it easy for them to get the ace of diamonds—for it is in the center.

Showing the fanned cards, he turns them faces down, making his slide and letting a spectator get the center card— one of the black aces.

"You didn't get the ace of diamonds?" comes the magician's question, as he drops the other two cards faces down on the table. "I'll tell you why. It's here!"

And he draws the missing ace of diamonds from his pocket!

17. THE HOAX WITH ACES   This is an old trick, but it is always a good one. It is performed with two aces—the red ones—and a confederate helps the magician.

The pack is divided into two packets. Upon one heap, the magician places the ace of hearts. He shows the ace of diamonds and puts it on the other heap. Lifting this heap he puts it on the ace of hearts, but as he does so, he quickly pulls the ace of diamonds from the top and drops it on the ace of hearts ahead of the descending packet.

The magician blandly states that the two aces will be found together. He deals cards from the bottom of the pack, turning them faces up, one by one. At last he comes to the first red ace. He states that the next card he draws off will be the other ace. Sure enough, it is.

Everyone laughs at the crudity of this trick and the confederate, with a wink at the audience, asks the magician to "do it again." The magician consents. But while he is showing the ace of diamonds to everyone, the confederate slyly takes a few cards from the upper heap and drops them on the ace of hearts.

Now, when the magician goes through his crude feat of slipping the ace of diamonds on to the lower heap, the laugh appears to be on him—for the aces will not be together.

The magician proceeds unwittingly, declaring that the two red aces will come together as he deals cards from the bottom. A red ace comes into view and the magician is emphatic that the next card will be the other ace. Everyone else laughs. So the magician brings forth the card and it actually is the missing ace!

Here is the method: The magician knows the card directly under the ace of hearts—say, the five of clubs. He knows what the confederate has done—that the aces will really be apart. But he deals away, pulling each card from the bottom and turning it face up until he sees the five of clubs. That tells him that the ace of hearts is next.

He does not deal the ace of hearts. Instead, he draws it back by means of the "glide"* and continues dealing other cards. The ace of diamonds comes up. To bring the ace of hearts next, the magician simply draws it forth, for it is on the bottom, waiting for him

18. THE IMPROVED ACE HOAX The effect of this trick is similar to the "Hoax with Aces." The magician shows how

*Described in Chapter Three.

he can make the red aces come together even though placed apart—but the crudity of his method fools no one.

Offering to do the trick again, he places the ace of hearts on one heap and shows the ace of diamonds. The confederate quickly seizes the ace of hearts and pockets it. The magician does not see the action.

The magician puts the ace of diamonds on top of the pack and makes the crude transfer, slipping it to the lower heap. When he says that the cards will come together—two red aces —no one believes him. But the magician has the last laugh, for the red aces come together and the confederate expresses surprise at finding a different card in his pocket.

In this case, the deception begins with the exhibition of the ace of hearts, before it is placed upon the lower half of the pack. The magician picks up the ace of hearts with another card on top of it. He shows these two cards as one; by bending the cards slightly outward, they hold firmly together and appear as one card.

Thus two cards go on the lower heap. While the magician is showing the ace of diamonds, the confederate quickly steals the top card of the lower heap. He does not have time to show its face. Everyone takes for granted that it is the ace of hearts. But the ace of hearts still remains on the lower heap.

So when the magician employs his crude maneuver, he actually brings the two aces together and he can deal the cards one by one from the bottom, arriving at the united aces.

In doing the trick in this form, the deal from the bottom is not essential. All through the trick, the magician can simply spread the pack face up and show the two aces side by side.

19. TRAVELING CARD TRICK The magician uses two envelopes and a pack of cards. He asks a spectator to count off twelve cards. The spectator does this. The magician then counts off twelve cards.

He verifies the spectator's count, counting the twelve cards again. He puts these twelve cards in one envelope. He seals the envelope. A spectator holds it.

The magician verifies the count of his own twelve cards. He puts his twelve in the other envelope. A spectator holds it—the envelope being sealed.

"Pass!" Three cards go from one envelope to the other. Nine in one envelope, fifteen in the other. Spectators open the envelopes themselves and do the counting!

Here's the method: Between the two envelopes the performer puts three cards, faces down. The envelopes are face to face. They are shown casually together. No one realizes that three cards are hidden between them.

A spectator counts off twelve cards and places them on the table. The performer counts off twelve—apparently—but actually he uses the "false count" and only counts off nine, making them appear as twelve.

When he verifies the spectator's count, he counts the cards upon the envelopes. He picks up the envelopes and lets the cards slide into his right hand. Needless to state, the hidden cards go with them. One envelope is dropped; the fifteen cards are sealed in the other.

The magician quickly verifies the count of his own cards, but he uses the elusive "false count" once more—so the packet which presumably contains twelve actually consists of nine cards. These are placed in the second envelope which is sealed. The rest is merely a matter of showmanship.

This trick is not at all difficult, but it should be presented convincingly. Afterward, spectators will believe they did all the counting themselves. Great importance should be attached to the fact that the sealed envelopes are held by the spectators.

Also, the magician should see to it that the envelopes look the same. He can ask for the spectators to select one. The magician then offers to make cards pass from it or into it—as the case may be. This should be done in a casual manner.

He can also ask for a number of cards—say between one and four—the response usually being "three." This makes it look as though the spectators decided upon the number that was to be used in the passing.

Should "two" be stated—the only other choice—the magician gets out of it by turning to another person and saying— "I wanted you to decide the number—but since two has been mentioned, we can use two—and one for you, which makes three altogether."

ABOUT THE AUTHOR

The name of Harry Blackstone (1885–1965) has been synonymous with magic for generations. Known as The Great Blackstone, he entertained thousands of American troops throughout the United States during World War II, and after the war resumed his tours of the larger cities of North America. He produced his own show books, magazine articles, radio program, and also wrote *Blackstone's Secrets of Magic* and *Blackstone's Magic Card Tricks*. His son, Harry Blackstone, Jr., was named America's Bicentennial Magician in 1976. Both performers have been awarded The Star of Magic, an honor bestowed only eleven times in eight decades. After a fifty-year career, Harry Blackstone retired to California in 1960.